Hampton-Brown

EDGE

CB

D1608902

NATIONAL GEOGRAPHIC LEARNING | CENGAGE Learning®

Acknowledgments

Grateful acknowledgment is given to the authors, artists, photographers, museums, publishers, and agents for permission to reprint copyrighted material. Every effort has been made to secure the appropriate permission. If any omissions have been made or if corrections are required, please contact the Publisher.

Photographic Credits

Cover: Avian Island, the Pantanal, Mato Grosso, Brazil, Mike Bueno. Photograph © Mike Bueno/National Geographic Stock.

For product information and technology asistance, contact us at
Cengage Learning Customer & Sales Support, 1-800-354-9706

For permission to use material from this text or product, submit all requests online at **www.cengage.com/permissions**
Further permissions questions can be emailed to
permissionrequest@cengage.com

National Geographic Learning | Cengage Learning
1 Lower Ragsdale Drive
Building 1, Suite 200
Monterey, CA 93940

Cengage Learning is a leading provider of customized learning solutions with office locations around the globe, including Singapore, the United Kingdom, Australia, Mexico, Brazil, and Japan. Locate your local office at **www.cengage.com/global**.

Visit National Geographic Learning online at **ngl.cengage.com**
Visit our corporate website at **www.cengage.com**

Printed in the USA.
RR Donnelley, Willard, OH

ISBN: 978-12857-34859 (Practice Book)
ISBN: 978-12857-34880 (Practice Book Teacher's Annotated Edition)

ISBN: 978-12857-67314 (Practice Masters)
Teachers are authorized to reproduce the practice masters in this book in limited quantity and solely for use in their own classrooms.

Printed in the United States of America
15 16 17 18 19 20 21 22
10 9 8 7 6 5 4 3

Contents

Contents, *continued*

UNIT 3

UNIT 4

Grammar: Possessives

Grammar: Prepositional Phrases

Grammar: Indefinite Pronouns

✔Edit and Proofread

UNIT 5

Grammar: Adjectives

Grammar: Comparisons

Contents, *continued*

UNIT 7

Grammar: Present Perfect Tense

Grammar: Perfect Tenses

Grammar: Participles and Participial Phrases

Proofreader's Marks

Mark	Meaning	Example
≡	Capitalize.	I love new york city.
/	Do not capitalize.	I'm going shopping at my favorite Store.
⊙	Add a period.	Mr͜͡ Lopez is our neighbor.
?	Add a question mark.	Where is my black pen
↓	Add an exclamation point.	Look out
＂Ｖ Ｖ＂	Add quotation marks.	You are late, said the teacher.
∧	Add a comma.	Amy how are you feeling today?
∧;	Add a semicolon.	This shirt is nice however, that one brings out the color of your eyes.
◇	Add a colon.	He wakes up at 6 30 a.m.
⊼	Add a dash.	Barney he's my pet dog has run away.
{ }	Add parentheses.	I want to work for the Federal Bureau of Investigation (FBI).
=	Add a hyphen.	You were born in mid=September, right?
Ｖ'	Add an apostrophe.	I m the oldest of five children.
#	Add a space.	She likes him alot.
◡	Close up a space.	How much home work do you have?
∧	Add text.	My keys are on the table.
℘	Delete.	I am going too my friend's house.
⌒℘	Change text.	We have too much garbage.
∩	Transpose words, letters.	Did you see thier new car?
ⓢⓟ	Spell out.	Today he is turning ⑯ ⓢⓟ
¶	Begin a new paragraph.	"I win!" I shouted ¶ "No, you don't," he said.
ⓘⓣⓐⓛ ___	Add italics.	The Spanish word for table is mesa. ⓘⓣⓐⓛ
ⓤ/ⓢ ___	Add underlining.	Little Women is one of my favorite books.

Name _____ Date _____

1 Are All Sentences the Same?

No. They Have Different Purposes.

Four Kinds of Sentences

1. Make a **statement** to tell something. End with a period.
   I can't decide what to do about my friend Bernie.

2. Ask a **question** to find out something. End with a question mark.
   Would you like to talk about it?

3. Use an **exclamation** to express a strong feeling. End with an exclamation point.
   Yes, I need help!

4. Give a **command** to tell someone what to do. End with a period.
   Stop worrying. Tell me about it. Don't leave anything out.

Start every sentence with a capital letter.

Try It

A. Read each sentence. Decide what kind of sentence it is. Write **statement**, **question**, **exclamation**, or **command** on the line.

1. What did Bernie do? ____question____

2. I think he cheated on the math test. _____

3. Don't tell anyone. _____

4. I can't believe it! _____

B. Change each sentence to the kind in parentheses. Use correct punctuation.

5. I saw Bernie get the answers from another student. **(question)** _Did you see Bernie get the answers from another student?_

6. Did you tell Mrs. Lynch about it? **(command)** _____

C. Answer the questions about a difficult choice you have made. Use at least two different kinds of sentences in your responses. Use correct punctuation.

7. What kind of choice did you make? I had to choose _____

_____.

8. Why was it difficult to make your choice? _____

_____

9. Did anyone help you make that choice? _____

_____

D. (10–14) Write at least five sentences to tell more about your choice. Vary the kinds of sentences in your response.

_____

_____

_____

_____

_____

Edit It

E. (15–20) Edit the journal entry. Fix the six mistakes. The first is done for you. Make sure to use correct punctuation for each kind of sentence.

December 10

I don't think our school does enough recycling⊙

I don't like that the cafeteria uses foam cups

Why don't they use paper cups and plates

I want to help the environment I'm just so

frustrated Should I complain to the principal

Proofreader's Marks

Add a period:

I am happy with my choices⊙

Add an exclamation point:

What a tough decision˅

Add a question mark:

How did you make your choice˅

See all Proofreader's Marks on page ix.

② What Do You Need for a Sentence?
A Subject and a Predicate

A complete sentence has two parts: the **subject** and the **predicate**.

subject	predicate

Kim plays baseball.

To find the parts, in most sentences, ask yourself:

1. Whom or what is the sentence about? Your answer is the **subject**. It may be one word or more than one word.

2. What does the subject do? Your answer is the **predicate**. Like the subject, the predicate may be one word or more than one.

Sentence	Whom or What?	What Does the Subject Do?
I joined the team.	I	joined the team
The coach gives me advice.	The coach	gives me advice

Try It

A. Match each subject with a predicate to make a complete sentence.

1. Our team ——————————— is one of the best teams around.

2. Mr. Harrison   coaches our team well.

3. All of his players   asks us to do our best.

4. He   work hard during practice.

5. The crowds   win lots of games!

6. We   cheer.

B. Choose a subject and a predicate from each column to make four sentences. Write the sentences on the lines. Use the words only once.

Subject	Predicate
One player	makes practice a priority now.
Coach Harrison	gave Harry one more chance.
The team	agreed with that decision.
Harry	missed practice often.

7. _One player missed practice often._

8. _____

9. _____

10. _____

Write It

C. Imagine your best friend is on a rival baseball team. When your team plays against his team, what do you do? Make sure you use a subject and a predicate in each sentence.

11. Do you hope he makes mistakes so your team can win? _I hope he_ _____
_____.

12. Is it hard to play against your friend? Why or why not? _____
_____

13. How do you think your friend feels about the issue? _____
_____

D. (14–18) Write at least five sentences to tell more about how you would handle the situation. Use subjects and predicates correctly.

_____

_____

_____

_____

_____

3 What Is a Sentence About?
The Subject

The **complete subject** can be one word or a phrase of several words. Zoom in on the most important word. Is it a noun? A **noun** is the name of a person, place, thing, or idea.

1. My **neighborhood** had trouble with telephone service last night.
2. A **storm** damaged the telephone lines.
3. The **wind** knocked down some trees.
4. My **friend** tried to call me.
5. **Liz** didn't know about the problem.
6. "The **problem** was the phone," I explained.

Nouns in the Subject	
Person	friend
	Liz
Place	neighborhood
Thing	storm
	wind
Idea	problem

Try It

A. Add a noun to complete the subject of the sentence.

1–2. My best _____friend_____ lives next door. His _____ is Sidney.

3. Our funniest _____ includes the day we met.

4. His _____ moved to our neighborhood last year.

5. My _____ decided to bake them cookies.

B. Complete each subject. Use the type of noun in parentheses.

6. _____I_____ offered to bring them the cookies. **(person)**

7. The _____ slipped out of my hand. **(thing)**

8. Their _____ was covered with cookies. **(place)**

9. The _____ made us laugh so hard our stomachs hurt! **(idea)**

C. Answer the questions about a good friend. Make sure each sentence has a subject.

10. Is your friend an old or a new friend? _____

11. How did you meet? _____

12. What do you like best about your friend? _____

_____

13. What do you think your friend likes about you? _____

_____

14. Does your friend ever help you? How? _____

_____

D. (15–19) Write at least five sentences to tell about things you and your friend enjoy doing together.

_____

_____

_____

_____

_____

Edit It

E. (20–25) Edit the article to include a complete subject. Fix the six mistakes.

Making Friends

Many students have trouble making friends. These can help ease the process. Look for with similar interests. A at school is a good start. Do like music? Sign up for chorus or band class. You can conquer your shyness. Shake and say hello. A new is worth the effort!

Proofreader's Marks

Add text:

friends
New are fun.
  ^

See all Proofreader's Marks on page ix.

④ What's the Most Important Word in the Predicate?

The Verb

- The **complete predicate** in a sentence often tells what the subject does. It can be one word or several words. The **verb** shows the action.

    We **talk** about the school election.

- Sometimes the predicate tells what the subject has. It uses these **verbs**:

    I **have** a friend named Janice.

    She **has** a good chance of winning.

- Other times, the predicate tells what the subject is or is like. The **verb** is a form of **be**.

    The school election **is** next week.

    We **are** great supporters of Janice.

    I **am** on the election committee.

Try It

A. Complete each predicate with a verb.

1. Our school _____ a president.

2. Every year we _____ for a new president.

3. I think Janice _____ a fine candidate.

4. Tim _____ everyone about Janice.

5. Janice _____ many friends at school.

6. Her friends _____ impressed with her.

7. I _____ for a good outcome.

8. Even Ben _____.

7

B. Choose words from each column to build five sentences about school elections. You can use words more than once.

Janice We Tim and Ben	is are need want	her to win. a good candidate. volunteers. a good school president.

9. _____

10. _____

11. _____

12. _____

13. _____

Write It

C. Answer the questions about school elections. Use verbs correctly.

14. Do your classmates get involved in school elections? _____

_____

15. What makes someone a good school president? _____

_____

D. (16–20) Write at least five sentences to tell why you would be a good school president. Use verbs correctly.

_____

_____

_____

_____

_____

5 Write Complete Sentences

Remember: You need a **subject** and a **predicate** to make a complete sentence. Often, the most important word in the subject is a **noun**. Every predicate needs a **verb**.

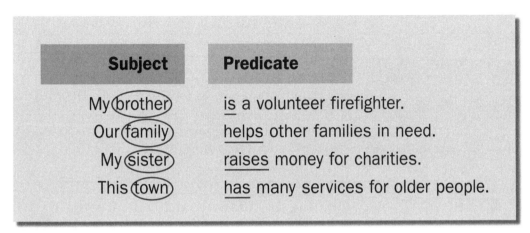

Subject	Predicate
My (brother)	<u>is</u> a volunteer firefighter.
Our (family)	<u>helps</u> other families in need.
My (sister)	<u>raises</u> money for charities.
This (town)	<u>has</u> many services for older people.

Try It

A. Add a subject, a verb, or a predicate to complete each sentence.

1. _____ need a helping hand.

2. _____ works at a homeless shelter.

3. _____ encourages me to help others.

4. I _____, too.

5. I _____ about the hospital.

6. The hospital _____ a good place to volunteer.

B. Circle the noun or pronoun in the subject and underline the verb in the predicate in each sentence.

7. My (parents) <u>set</u> a good example for me.

8. Their choices are usually logical.

9. I follow their example.

10. My family talks about my decisions.

Write It

C. Answer the questions about how you make decisions. Use complete sentences.

11. How do family members help you make decisions? Sometimes _____ help

_____.

12. Who gives you the best advice? _____

13. Do you make some choices on your own? _____

14. Do you consider all the facts carefully when you make a decision? _____

_____

D. (15–18) Write at least four sentences to tell about how you make good decisions. Make sure each sentence includes both a subject and a predicate.

_____

_____

_____

_____

_____

Edit It

E. (19–25) Edit the list. Fix the seven mistakes to make complete sentences.

Rules to Live By

1. I always use good judgment.
2. I decisions logically.
3. First, think carefully about the facts.
4. Second, I about the consequences.
5. Then I to trustworthy people.
6. I to others.
7. Finally, I the right thing.
8. That my way of doing things.

Proofreader's Marks

Add text:

I always think carefully.

See all Proofreader's Marks on page ix.

10   © National Geographic Learning, a part of Cengage Learning, Inc.

6 What's a Plural Noun?

A Word That Names More Than One Thing

One	More Than One
A **singular noun** names one thing.	A **plural noun** names more than one thing.

Use these spelling rules for forming plural nouns.

1. To make most nouns plural, just add -**s**.

2. If the noun ends in **s**, **z**, **sh**, **ch**, or **x**, add -**es**.

3. If the noun ends in **y** after the consonant, change the **y** to **i** and add -**es**.

4. Some nouns have special plural forms.

One	More Than One
choice	choices
box	boxes
family	families
child	children
person	people

Try It

A. (1–4) Read these nouns: **classes, fly, plans, dish**. Which nouns are singular and which are plural? Put each noun in the correct column. Then add its other form. The first one is done for you.

Singular Nouns (one)	Plural Nouns (more than one)
class	classes

B. Write the plural form of the singular noun in parentheses.

5. Some _____ are influenced by their peers. **(child)**

6. They do not make _____ on their own. **(decision)**

7. To be accepted, they might do things that go against their true _____. **(wish)**

C. Answer the questions about who or what influences your choices.
Use singular and plural nouns in your response.

8. Who influences your decisions the most? I am influenced the most by _____

_____.

9. Do you feel pressure to be like other students? _____

10. Are you influenced by outside sources, like people you see on television or in the movies?

_____

_____

D. (11–14) Write at least four sentences to tell more about who or what influences your
choices. Use at least two singular nouns and two plural nouns in your response.

_____

_____

_____

E. (15–20) Edit the journal entry. Fix the six mistakes. Make sure you use the
correct noun form for each sentence.

February 16
I am determined to make my own decisions.
Certain studentes at my school try to
convince other peoples to make poor choice.
They encourage them to smoke or drink.
Sometimes I even see very young childrens
with cigarettes. These boies and girls do not
really want to smoke. They just go along
with the crowd to be popular. I wish more
person would think for themselves!

Proofreader's Marks

Change text:
Many child are not so
lucky.

children

See all Proofreader's Marks
on page ix.

7 How Do You Know What Verb to Use?

Match It to the Subject.

- Use **I** with **am**.
  I am in the school auditorium.

- Use **he**, **she**, or **it** with **is**.
  It is filled with students. A guest **speaker is** on stage.
  He is a professional athlete.

- Use **we**, **you**, or **they** with **are**.
  My **friends are** athletes, too. **They are** fans of the speaker.
  We are curious about his life. **Are you?**

Forms of *Be*
I **am**
he, she, or it **is**
we, you, or they **are**

Try It

A. Complete each sentence about a role model. Use am, is, or are.

1. The guest speaker _____ from my neighborhood.

2. He _____ able to inspire teens. He uses his life story as an example.

3. He knows it _____ not easy to study, work, and play sports.

4. "Coaches and teachers can help," he says. "They _____ on your side."

5. I _____ confident that I can achieve my dream with hard work.

B. (6–11) Read the interview. Write am, is, or are on each line.

Q. Who _____ your role model?

A. My dad _____ my role model. I _____ proud of how hard he works.
He _____ now a business owner. My mom shares the responsibilities. They
_____ happy about the business.

Q. Describe one trait that you and your dad share. How are you the same?

A. We _____ both impatient! We always try to finish things quickly.

C. Answer the questions about yourself and your role model.

12. What are your talents? I _____ good at _____.

13. What is one goal you have? My goal _____ to _____.

14. Who is your role model? _____

15. How is this person a good role model? _____

_____

D. (16–19) Write at least four sentences to tell more about yourself and your role model.

_____

_____

_____

_____

_____

Edit It

E. (20–25) Edit the journal entry. Fix the six mistakes.

> March 31
>
> I think hard work is the best way to achieve my goal. My dreams is big. I are dedicated. My friends is not always as serious. They is not worried about money, college, or jobs. However, I choose to work and study. My family am helpful. Together, we be a team. My sister is a good example. She is a success already.

Proofreader's Marks

Change text:
                  are
We ~~is~~ successful.

See all Proofreader's Marks on page ix.

(8) How Do You Know What Action Verb to Use?
Match It to the Subject.

- **Action verbs** tell when a subject does something, like **ride**, **look**, or **drive**. If the sentence is about one other person, place, or thing, add **-s** to the action verb.

  1. My sisters **ride** the bus.   **2.** Our cousin **rides** the bus, too.

  3. We **look** out the window.   **4.** A driver **looks** at us.

  5. My parents **drive** the car.   **6.** Dad **drives** us to the store.

- If there is more than one action verb in a sentence, all verbs must agree with the subject:

  My neighbor **drives**, **parks**, and **locks** his car.

Try It

A. Complete each sentence about money. Write the correct verb.

1. My parents _____*give*_____ me money for lunch at school.
      give / gives

2. I _____ to earn my own spending money.
      need / needs

3. My sisters _____ after school.
      work / works

4. I _____ many reasons for spending money.
      find / finds

5. I _____ a little money each week.
      save / saves

6. My mom _____ me to save for an emergency or for a vacation.
      ask / asks

7. I _____ on the weekends.
      work / works

8. My friends call me, _____ to go out, and forget that I need money.
      ask / asks

9. I decide to stay home. My sister _____ home with me.
      stay / stays

B. Choose words from each column to build six sentences about getting a ride to school. You can use words more than once.

Teresa	asks	an extra shift.
She	owns	a car.
I	want	for gas money.
	ask	for a ride.
	work	

10. _____

11. _____

12. _____

13. _____

14. _____

15. _____

Write It

C. Your friend at work adds extra hours to her timesheet. You want to earn more money, too. Do you add more hours to your timesheet, or do you tell the store owner?

16. Do you think adding extra time is right? I _____

_____.

17. How does your friend cause a problem for you? She _____

_____

_____.

D. (18–20) Write at least three sentences to tell more about your choice. Use action verbs correctly.

_____

_____

_____

_____

⑨ What's a Compound Subject?

It's a Subject with Two or More Nouns.

When a subject has two or more nouns joined by **and** or **or**, it is called a **compound subject**.

1. **Adults and children** help our community.
2. **Henry and Fiona** plan a fundraiser.
3. A **book sale or** a **cake sale** makes money.
4. The **parents or** the **school** needs to help.
5. The **school or** the **parents** need to help.

How do you know what verb to use with a compound subject?

- If you see **and**, use a plural verb like **help** or **plan**.
- If you see **or**, look at the last noun in the subject. Is it singular? Then use a singular verb. Is it plural? Then use a plural verb.

Try It

A. Write the correct form of the verb in parentheses.

1. My classmates and our community _____ together to make
   work / works
   our town beautiful.

2. The bank and the grocery store _____ money for a new park.
   donate / donates

3. Parents and teens _____ trees.
   plant / plants

4. The mayor and police officers _____, too.
   help / helps

5. An adult or teens _____ shovels.
   bring / brings

6. My friends and my classmates _____ the new plants.
   water / waters

7. The parents or the school _____ photos.
   take / takes

B. Complete each sentence with a compound subject to match the verb.

8. _____ and _____ volunteer at the local hospital.

9. My _____ and my _____ volunteer there, too.

10. The _____ and the _____ keep my brother and sister busy.

11. Both _____ and _____ love to see them.

12. _____ or _____ visits every Saturday.

Write It

C. Answer the questions about community service. Use compound subjects correctly.

13. What do you do to help at home or at school? _____

_____

14. What accomplishments are you proud of? _____

_____

_____

15. Which two places in your community would you most like to volunteer? _____

_____

_____

D. (16–20) Write at least five sentences to tell why you would choose to do community service. Make sure you use at least two compound subjects.

_____

_____

_____

_____

_____

_____

🔟 Make Subjects and Verbs Agree

Remember: The verb you use depends on your subject. These subjects and verbs go together:

Forms of *Be*	**Action Verbs**
I **am** interested.	I **join** the club.
You **are** interested.	You **join** the club, too.
He, she, or it **is** interested.	He, she, or it **joins** the club.
We, you, or they **are** interested.	We, you, or they **join** the club.
My friends **are** interested.	Teenagers **join** the club.
My friends and I **are** interested.	My friends and I **join** the club.

Try It

A. Complete each sentence about careers. Write the verb that goes with the subject.

1. My friend Ana and I _____ the career club.
   join / joins

2. Ana _____ to study business.
   want / wants

3. She _____ interested in marketing.
   is / are

4. I _____ interested in a career in health.
   is / am

5. I also _____ to study large animals.
   want / wants

B. Write the correct form of the verb in parentheses.

6. John and Bianca _____ about careers at the library. **(read)**

7. John _____ to be a pilot. **(hope)**

8. He _____ a pilot on career day. **(meet)**

9. John _____ to the pilot about his career choice. **(talk)**

C. Answer the questions about your future career. Make sure your subjects and verbs agree.

10. What careers are you interested in? I _____ interested in _____

_____.

11. Do you know anyone who works in one of these careers? What do they do? _____

_____

12. What would you like to ask them about their career? I _____

_____.

D. (13–15) Write at least three sentences to tell more about a career you would like to choose. Make sure each verb agrees with its subject.

_____

_____

_____

_____

Edit It

E. (16–20) Edit the letter. Fix the five mistakes with verbs.

Dear Aunt Dorothy,

    I think about my future a lot these days. Yesterday, we had Career Day at school. Now I has lots of information about different careers. I met a research scientist. She are very excited about her job. She make important decisions every day. I am interested in a career in science. I are also quite interested in a career in music. That is why I am writing to you. Do you like your career? Is you happy as a professional guitarist?

Love,

Marina

Proofreader's Marks

Change text:
        is
She ~~are~~ successful.

See all Proofreader's Marks on page ix.

⑪ What Is a Fragment?

It's an Incomplete Sentence.

A **fragment** is a group of words that begins with a capital letter and ends with a period. It looks like a sentence, but it is not complete. A subject or a verb may be missing.

Fragments	Sentences
1. Moves to a new town.	Tina moves to a new town.
2. She the school.	She likes the school.
3. The teens in the park.	The teens meet in the park.
4. Makes new friends.	She makes new friends.

Try It

A. Write whether each group of words is a fragment or a sentence. If it is a fragment, add a subject or a verb. Write the complete sentence.

1. Jason to a new school. _fragment; Jason goes to a new school._

_____

2. Students at the new school study hard. _____

_____

3. Decides to study harder this year. _____

_____

B. (4–8) Each group of words in the paragraph is a fragment. Add a subject or a verb to complete each sentence.

Everyone _____ sports at my new school. All of the students

_____ to play on a team. My old _____ was different. Most

_____ there did not play sports. I _____ glad to be here

because I love sports!

Write It

C. Answer the questions about your school. Use complete sentences in your response.

9. What do you like best about your school? My favorite _____
_____.

10. Do you and your classmates share many of the same interests? _____
_____

11. Do you think a new student would feel welcome at your school? Why or why not? _____
_____

D. (12–14) Write at least three sentences that would give a new student a good idea of what your school is like. Read your sentences aloud. Fix any fragments you might hear.

_____

_____

_____

_____

_____

Edit It

E. (15–20) Edit the letter. Fix the six fragments. Add a subject or a verb.

Dear Samantha,

You are on my mind today. I miss seeing you at school. This school is different from our school back in Oklahoma. The here are very full and noisy. I to fit in. It not always easy. A is helping me. Her is Clarisse. She encourages me to join the chorus. I to sing. I guess it is good to try new things!

Your friend,

Marion

Proofreader's Marks

Add text:
make
They ᶺ friends easily.

See all Proofreader's Marks on page ix.

12 What's One Way to Fix a Fragment?

Add a Subject.

- A complete sentence has a **subject** and a **predicate**.
- To check for a subject, ask yourself:
  Whom or what is the sentence about?

Fragments	Sentences
1. Reads a magazine.	**Charlene** reads a magazine.
2. Sees a picture of a dress she likes.	**She** sees a picture of a dress she likes.
3. Buys the dress.	**She** buys the dress.
4. Says Charlene looks like a movie star.	**Maya** says Charlene looks like a movie star.

Try It

A. (1–5) Fix the five fragments. Add a subject to make a complete sentence.

Premiere Soap Promises a Flawless Complexion
Premiere Soap is used by real TV stars. Makes your skin feel as soft as silk. Many people across the nation buy it. See amazing results. Find that their skin improves within days. Actress Sadie Chanelle uses Premiere Soap. Has a flawless complexion. Can, too! Try our soap for five days. You will see results.

Proofreader's Marks

Do not capitalize:

The A̸ctress is talented.

Add text:
            are
Movies ᵔ exciting.

See all Proofreader's Marks on page ix.

B. **(6–10)** Draw a line from each subject to the correct predicate.

6. I	saw a new product on television.
7. It	buy those sneakers.
8. All my friends	think the sneakers look cool.
9. They	is a pair of sneakers that light up.
10. My brother	says he thinks they look stupid.

Write It

C. Answer the questions about the influence of TV, movies, and magazines on you and your peers. Make sure each sentence has a subject.

11. Are you influenced by the behavior of famous actors? I _____

_____.

12. Do you buy certain products because they are advertised on television? _____

_____

13. Which celebrity do you admire the most? _____

_____

14. What qualities do you admire in this person? _____

_____

15. Are many of your friends influenced by celebrities? How? _____

_____

D. **(16–20)** Write at least five sentences. Tell how your choices and actions are influenced by specific people you read about in magazines or see on television or in movies. Then read your sentences aloud. Fix any fragments.

_____

_____

_____

_____

_____

_____

13 What's Another Way to Fix a Fragment?

Add a Predicate, and Be Sure It Has a Verb.

When you write a sentence, be sure to include the verb. If you leave out the verb, the words you wrote are a **fragment**. Study the sentences in the chart.

Fragments	Sentences
1. Josh his older brother.	Josh **admires** his older brother.
2. He the Best Track Athlete award.	He **won** the Best Track Athlete award.
3. Josh a medal, too.	Josh **wants** a medal, too.
4. He each morning.	He **runs** each morning.

Try It

A. (1–5) Fix the five fragments. Add a verb to make a complete sentence.

July 5
My friend Ben creates beautiful paintings. He a terrific artist. I to learn to paint, too. Ben he will teach me. I eager to get started on a picture. I my dog King should be my first model!

Proofreader's Marks

Add text:
Artists ∧ fun.
      have

See all Proofreader's Marks on page ix.

B. Complete each sentence with a verb.

6. Harry _____ the piano.

7. Harry's brother _____ a concert pianist.

8. Harry _____ hard at his lessons.

9. He _____ to play as well as his brother.

C. Think about friends and family that you admire. Have their successes influenced the way you think about your own personal goals? Write complete sentences.

10. Who do you admire? I admire _____

_____.

11. How has their example influenced your own personal goals? _____

_____

_____

D. (12–15) Write at least four sentences to tell more about your personal goals. Then read your sentences aloud. Fix any fragments you might hear.

_____

_____

_____

_____

_____

_____

Edit It

E. (16–20) Edit the journal entry below. Fix the five fragments. Add a verb to form a complete sentence.

April 22

I am very happy with my project. I a weekly study group at my house. It like the one Uncle Charlie used to have. My friends and I better grades now. Each group member in charge of one subject. I sure everyone understands math.

Proofreader's Marks

Add text:
likes
Louise ∧ math.

14 What's One More Way to Fix a Fragment?

Combine Neighboring Sentences.

Writers may create a fragment by starting a new sentence when they shouldn't. These fragments are easy to fix. Just combine the fragment with the sentence before it.

          ⌐——— sentence ———⌐ ⌐——— fragment ———⌐
1. Irina used to set the table. While her father cooked dinner.
Irina used to set the table while her father cooked dinner.

          ⌐——— sentence ———⌐ ⌐——— fragment ———⌐
2. Now Irina cooks dinner. Because her father is busy.
Now Irina cooks dinner because her father is busy.

A. Find each fragment. Combine it with the other sentence and write the new sentence.

1. Irina's sister is a role model for her. Because she is so intelligent. _____

_____

2. Irina wanted to be a nurse like her sister. When she was younger. _____

_____

3. Now she has other ideas. Because she learned about more careers. _____

_____

4. She learned about new careers. When she attended Career Day at school. _____

_____

5. She is considering a career in law. Or studying finance. _____

_____

6. Her father is a lawyer. And works at a law firm. _____

_____

B. Rewrite each sentence by adding a fragment from the box. Punctuate your sentences correctly.

Because her interests have changed.	And speaks Spanish.
Who is a teacher.	Because his brother is one.

7. John wants to be an electrician. _John wants to be an electrician because his brother is one._

8. Gretchen is influenced by her sister. _____

_____

9. Kate's mother is from Ecuador. _____

_____

10. Tina doesn't know what to do. _____

_____

Write It

C. Complete each sentence with your own ideas and beliefs about how you and your interests have changed over time. Use complete sentences.

11. I used to enjoy _____.

12. I was interested in that because _____.

13. Now I prefer to _____.

14. My interest changed because _____.

15. Another way I have changed is _____.

D. (16–20) Write at least five sentences to tell more about how you and your interests have changed. Then read your sentences aloud. Fix any fragments.

_____

_____

_____

_____

_____

15 Fix Sentence Fragments

Remember: You can fix a fragment by adding a subject or predicate that includes a verb. Or, you can combine the fragment with another sentence.

Fragment:	Tells Ella about the race.
Sentence:	Bonnie tells Ella about the race.
Fragment:	Bonnie Ella to try to win.
Sentence:	Bonnie wants Ella to try to win.
Fragment:	Ella is not sure. If she wants to enter the race.
Sentence:	Ella is not sure if she wants to enter the race.

Try It

A. Fix the fragments and write complete sentences.

1. Is a big influence on Juan. _____

2. Juan. _____

3. Juan listens carefully to Kevin. Because he has good ideas. _____
   _____

4. Thinks things over, but he makes his own decisions. _____
   _____

B. Each group of words is a fragment. Add a subject or a verb or combine the fragment with the other sentence. Write the complete sentence.

5. Had to make a choice. _____

6. David me advice. _____

7. Had a similar experience. _____

8. His comments were helpful. Because he has a lot of experience. _____
   _____

C. Answer the questions about a decision you have made. Make sure your sentences are complete. Include a subject and a predicate with a verb.

9. What was a big decision you have made? I decided to _____

_____.

10. What advice did you get? _____

_____

11. Did you do what they suggested? Why or why not? _____

_____

D. (12–15) Write at least four sentences to tell more about your decision. What other influences did you consider when you made your decision? Then read your sentences aloud. Fix any fragments.

_____

_____

_____

_____

_____

Edit It

E. (16–20) Edit the advice letter. Fix five mistakes.

Dear Chris,

I am glad you asked for my advice about your friend. Have a difficult decision to make. Think you should tell your friend the truth. A good friendship based on honesty. And honesty is so important. That is just my opinion. You have to decide. What seems right to you.

Your cousin,

Andy

Proofreader's Marks
Delete:
I know what to do now.
Do not capitalize:
They Told me.
Add text: is
It my idea.
See all Proofreader's Marks on page ix.

Name __Citlaly Magallon__   Date __02/13/20__

✓ Capitalize Proper Nouns and Adjectives

Proper nouns are capitalized because they name specific people, places, and things. Common nouns, which are general, are not capitalized.

Common Noun	Proper Noun
principal	Principal Edwards
state	Florida

Proper adjectives, which come from proper nouns, are also capitalized.

Proper Noun	Proper Adjective
Japan	Japanese
Boston	Bostonian

Try It

A. Use proofreader's marks to correct the capitalization error in each sentence.

1. My mom and I went to our favorite italian restaurant to talk about our big move.

2. We had to decide which City we would move to, Chicago or Miami.

3. I had never been to Chicago, but I had been to illinois.

4. I decided to look at a map of the United states.

Proofreader's Marks

Capitalize:
  My mother is from japan.

Do not capitalize:
  I like Japanese Food.

See all Proofreader's Marks on page ix.

B. (5–11) Edit the journal entry. Fix the seven mistakes. The first is done for you.

> My mom suggested I do more research about
> each City. I looked in a miami Newspaper.
> There was an article about a new Art school.
> It is the best one in the State. They have
> special programs in latin music and asian art.

✔ Punctuate Quotations Correctly

- Use quotation marks (" ") around the exact words that people speak. Do not use quotation marks when you describe what people said.

  Quotation: "I made my choice," I said to my mom.

  Description: I told my mom that I made my choice.

- Use a comma to set off **tags**, or words that identify who is quoted.

  She replied, "I'm glad that you made your choice."

  "I'm glad that you made your choice," **she replied**.

  "I'm glad," **she replied**, "that you made your choice."

Try It

A. Edit each sentence. Add or delete quotation marks and commas.

12. "She said that we didn't have to move if I didn't want to."

13. I replied, "I'm ready for a fresh start."

14. "A fresh start" she said, "would be good for both of us."

15. I told my mom, "everything I found out about each city."

16. Then I said," Miami has a new art school."

17. My mom asked, "Is it expensive?"

18. I replied, "Maybe I can get a scholarship."

19. She said, "That would be perfect."

Proofreader's Marks
Add quotation marks: My mom said, ˇPick the city that will make you happy.
Add comma: "Thank you" I replied.
Delete: She said we could go.

B. Rewrite the following descriptive sentences so that they include quotations.

20. My mom told me to send in my application. My mom said, "send your application".

21. I told her I sent it in yesterday. I said, "I sent it yesterday"

✔ Check Your Spelling

Homonyms are words that sound alike but have different meanings and spellings. Spell these homonyms correctly when you proofread.

Homonyms and Their Meanings	Examples
it's (contraction) = it is; it has	**It's** scary to apply to a new school.
its (adjective) = belonging to it	The school made **its** decision.
there (adverb) = that place or position	I got accepted. I'm going **there**.
their (adjective) = belonging to them	The teachers like **their** new theater.
they're (contraction) = they are	**They're** happy to have a new student.

Try It

A. Use proofreader's marks to correct the homonym errors.

22. Our neighbors are moving, too. ~~Their~~ *They're* moving to Boston.

23. ~~There~~ *Their* new house is bigger than the one they live in now.

24. We are going ~~their~~ *There* to visit them in the fall.

25. ~~Its~~ *It's* beautiful in the city at that time of the year.

26. The city has ~~it's~~ *its* apple festival in the fall.

Proofreader's Marks

Change text:
~~Their~~ *There* are two cities we like.

B. (27–32) Complete the story. Add a correct homonym to each sentence.

I was excited about the art school, and I immediately began to fantasize about going ___there___. ___It's___ the best art school in the state. I read more about the school online. ___their___ theater program includes field trips to Broadway plays. ___They're___ accepting applications now for next year. The school sends ___its___ response in June. ___It's___ so hard to wait!

Name _____ Date _____

✓ Check Sentences for Completeness

A sentence is complete when it expresses a complete thought and has two parts: the **subject** and the **predicate**. A **subject** tells who. A **predicate** tells what the subject does. Every predicate needs a **verb**.

Problem	Solution
1. **Sentence is missing a subject.** Received a promotion.	**Add the missing subject.** She received a promotion.
2. **Sentence is missing a verb.** Her boss happy with her work.	**Add the missing verb.** Her boss was happy with her work.
3. **Fragments are not sentences.** He wanted her to open a new branch office. In Miami.	**Join the fragments.** He wanted her to open a new branch office in Miami.

Try It

A. Match each subject to the correct predicate to form a complete sentence.

33. My mom and I   gave her a promotion.

34. Then she   ate at our favorite restaurant.

35. Her boss   were opening a new office in Miami.

36. The company   was expanding.

37. They   told me the big news.

Proofreader's Marks

Delete text and do not capitalize:

I gave her₰The full presentation.

Add text:

    was
Mom ᰂglad about her promotion.

B. (38–40) Edit the journal entry. Fix the three incomplete sentences.

January 23

She told me we didn't have to move if I didn't want to. I wasn't sure if I wanted. To move or not. Went online to find out more about Miami. This not an easy decision.

© National Geographic Learning, a part of Cengage Learning, Inc.

16 Is the Subject of a Sentence Always a Noun?

No, It Can Be a Pronoun.

- Use **I** when you talk about yourself.

  I love to paint. **I** want to take classes to learn more about it.

- Use **you** when you talk to another person.

  You learned to play the drums at a very young age.

- Use **he** when you talk about one man or one boy.

  My father is a comic book artist. **He** began drawing in high school.

- Use **she** when you talk about one woman or one girl.

  My aunt likes to write. **She** writes poems for a magazine.

- Use **it** when you talk about one place, thing, or idea.

  My brother wrote a song. **It** has a great rhythm.

Subject Pronouns
Singular
I
you
he, she, it

Try It

A. Complete each sentence. Use a subject pronoun from the chart.

1. Creativity can be developed through many activities. _____It_____ makes the world interesting and exciting.

2. Phillip is a wonderful writer. _____He_____ wrote an excellent story.

3. The story was about flying an airplane. _____I_____ was very exciting to read.

4. My favorite hobby is singing. _____I_____ sing almost every day.

5. Mayalinn painted a picture of a flying saucer. _____She_____ have to see it to believe it!

6. I told the artist, "_____You_____ are very talented."

7. My mother is creative. _____She_____ paints beautiful murals.

B. (8–14) Complete each sentence with a subject pronoun from the box.

She	He	It	I	You

My older sister Julia is a dancer. _____ began dancing when she was five years old. My father saw that she had talent. _____ signed Julia up for dance lessons. After high school, Julia went to a special institute for dancers. There, _____ danced in shows. A man from a theater company saw one of the shows. _____ asked my sister to join his theater. She accepted. Now Julia travels with many dancers across the country. Her job is demanding. _____ requires a lot of hard work, but Julia loves it. I see several of her shows each year. _____ am proud of my sister. _____ would be impressed with her dancing, too.

Write It

C. Answer the questions about creative talents. Use complete sentences and subject pronouns.

15. What is your talent? _____ am talented at _____
_____.

16. Who helped you realize you had this talent? _____ helped me. _____
told me that _____.

17. What steps can you take to develop your talent? _____
_____
_____

D. (18–20) Write at least three sentences about creative people in your family.
Use subject pronouns in your sentences.

_____
_____
_____
_____
_____
_____

Name _____ Date _____

17 Can a Pronoun Show "More Than One"?
Yes, It Can.

- Use **we** to talk about yourself and another person.

  My friends and I wrote a play.

  We will act it out on Friday.

- Use **you** to talk to one or more persons.

  You like our school plays, don't you?

  You should all be there on Friday.

- Use **they** to talk about more than one person or thing.

  Many other students helped us.

  They wanted to help tell the story.

Subject Pronouns	
Singular	**Plural**
I	we
you	you
he, she, it	they

Try It

A. Read the first sentence. Complete the second sentence with the correct subject pronoun.

1. My friends and I love acting. _____ wrote a play.

2. Our play is about a boy named José. _____ came from El Salvador at age seven.

3. His teachers notice that José has creative talent. _____ praise his writing.

4. When José's mother reads his stories, _____ knows that he will become a famous writer.

5. We will perform our play at school. _____ will be a hit!

6. I would like you to go. _____ should plan on attending.

7. You should bring your friends. _____ will enjoy it.

8. I will send you an invitation. _____ should respond by Friday.

B. Draw a line from the first sentence to the one that logically follows. Be sure the subject nouns and pronouns match.

9. My younger sister is very creative.

10. The art teacher got my sister involved in drawing for school.

11. Students saw her drawings and complimented her.

12. My parents thought my sister could find more creative outlets.

13. The directors of a local day care wanted an artist to help paint murals on the walls.

14. My parents and I suggested that my sister go to an art institute after high school.

They admired her skills.

We believe she can have a career as an artist.

He asked her to draw a cartoon for the school paper.

They helped her find other ways to use her skills in the community.

She took an art class and found that she had talent for drawing and painting.

They asked my sister to paint a picture in each room.

Write It

C. Answer the questions about a creative project you would like to participate in. Use subject pronouns where needed.

15. What creative project would you like to participate in? _____ would like to

_____.

16. Whom would you like to work with? _____ would like to work with _____.

17. What role would the other person have? _____ would help _____.

18. Who would your audience be? _____

19. How would having a partner make a difference to the project? _____

D. (20–25) Write at least six sentences that tell more about what each person would bring to the project. Use subject pronouns.

_____

_____

_____

_____

_____

_____

18 Can a Compound Subject Include a Pronoun?

Yes, and the Pronoun Comes Last.

A **compound subject** can include nouns and pronouns joined by **and** or **or**.

1. **My brother and I** need an art studio. We ask our mother what to do.
2. **My father and she** suggest we fix up the attic.
3. **My brother and I** want to use the space for painting and sculpting.
4. **He and I** are very excited about the new room.
5. First, **our parents or we** need to clean out the attic.

How do you know where to place the pronoun?

- Nouns always come before pronouns.
- The pronoun **I** always comes last.

Try It

A. Complete each sentence. Write the correct compound subject.

1. _____ have many ideas for our attic studio.
   I and my brother / My brother and I

2. _____ will make a list of things we need for the new room.
   We and our friends / Our friends and we

3. My friend Antonio has a truck. _____ will pick up the truck.
   My brother or he / He or my brother

4. _____ will check the carpet store for old scraps.
   I and my friend / My friend and I

B. (5–8) Complete each sentence about a project. Use compound subjects with a pronoun and the word **and**.

My parents decided to improve the backyard. My uncle _____ did most of the work. My uncle started right away. My father _____ removed the concrete walk. In its place, we decided to put small stones. My sister _____ did that. My sister wanted to plant flowers. My father _____ planted daisies.

Write It

C. Answer the questions about improving your bedroom. Use simple or compound subjects.

9. Why did you want to change your bedroom? _____ wanted to change my bedroom because _____.

10. What changes did you decide to make? _____ decided to _____ _____.

11. Who helped you? _____ helped me. _____ helped by _____ _____.

12. How did your changes improve your room? _____

D. (13–15) Write at least three sentences about a project you did with others to improve your home. Use simple and compound subjects.

_____

_____

_____

Edit It

E. (16–20) Edit the journal entry. Fix the five pronoun mistakes.

May 26

My friend Martha helped me decorate my room. I and Martha worked for hours. My parents and us love the result! Martha's father gave me some shelves. I wonder how Martha and him fit them into their car. The shelves look spectacular in my room. My brother or me will take a photograph. Now my brother's friends and are fixing his room.

Proofreader's Marks

Transpose words:

⌒I and Bo⌒ painted my room.

Add text:
                    |
My brother and ʌhung posters.   ʌ

Change text:
        I
He or ~~me~~ will take a photo. ʌ

See all Proofreader's Marks on page ix.

19 How Do You Avoid Confusion with Pronouns?

Match the Pronoun to the Noun.

If you're not sure which **pronoun** to use, first find the **noun**
it goes with. Then ask yourself:

- Is the noun a man, a woman, or a thing?
  Use **he** for a man, **she** for a woman, and **it** for a thing.

- Is the noun singular or plural? If plural, use **we**, **you**, or **they**.

If a pronoun does not refer correctly to a noun, change the pronoun.

Incorrect: All of the **students** make pictures for the fundraiser.
He work very hard.

Correct: All of the **students** make pictures for the fundraiser.
They work very hard.

The pronouns in these sentences are correct. Do you know why?

1. **Students** need a new writing lab at school. **They** decide to
    have a fundraiser.

2. The **fundraiser** will be next week. **It** will be a carnival.

Try It

A. Complete the sentence with a pronoun that matches the underlined word or words.

1. The <u>students</u> in school play on old equipment. _____ need new equipment.

2. <u>My classmates and I</u> want to help. _____ ask to have a fundraiser.

3. We ask <u>Ms. Ruiz</u> for help. _____ decides to ask the school board.

4. Ms. Ruiz describes our plan to the <u>members</u>. _____ give us permission.

B. (5–8) Complete the sentences with correct pronouns.

Our class took a field trip to an art exhibit. _____ loved the artwork.

_____ was a great trip. Thanh and Marie's favorite painting was of a little

boy. _____ thought it looked so lifelike. I am so glad that my classmates

and I went to the museum. _____ learned a lot about the art.

C. Answer the questions about an art event you attended. Use pronouns correctly.

9. What type of art event did you attend? _____ attended _____.

10. Who went with you? _____ and _____ went to the event.

11. Why did you go? _____

12. What did you do or see there? _____

13. How did you and your friends feel about the event? _____

_____

14. Would you recommend this event to others? Why or why not? _____

_____

D. (15–16) Write at least two sentences that tell more about this or another art event you attended. Use pronouns correctly.

_____

_____

_____

_____

E. (17–20) Edit the letter. Fix the four mistakes in pronouns.

Dear Chelsey,

   I want to invite you to a music festival on Sunday. Would she like to go with me? A few of our other friends are going, too. would meet them there. Musicians from Honduras are playing. He are bringing special instruments. If we get hungry, don't worry. She can buy lunch at a food stand there. I hope you can go!

Your friend,

Chris

Proofreader's Marks

Change text:

You
~~It~~ should go.

Add text:

   she
She said ⌄ will go.

See all Proofreader's Marks on page ix.

20 Use Subject Pronouns

Remember: The subject of a sentence can be a pronoun. A **subject pronoun** can be singular or plural.

- Use **I** when you talk about yourself.
- Use **you** to talk to one or more persons.
- Use **we** to talk about another person and yourself.
- Use **he**, **she**, **it**, and **they** to talk about other people or things.

  How do you know which pronoun to use? Look at the noun it goes with.
  1. If the noun is a man or boy, use **he**. If it is a woman or girl, use **she**.
  2. If the noun is a place or thing, use **it**. If the noun is plural, use **they**.

Try It

A. Complete each sentence. Write the correct subject pronoun.

1. Franco made a project for class. _____ worked on it for months.
   He / They

2. Sheila gave good advice. _____ said the project should be unique.
   He / She

3. Many students entered the science fair. _____ all worked hard.
   They / It

4. Franco's project was interactive. _____ thinks that added creativity.
   She / He

B. (5–9) Read the interview. Complete each sentence with the correct pronoun.

Q. How did you make your project the most creative at the science fair?

A. First, I chose an interesting subject. Then, my friend Sheila gave me advice.

_____ said my project should stand out. The other students and I discussed

creative ideas. _____ thought of many ways to make projects unique. I

decided to make my project an interactive experiment. The judges spent a long time at

my display. _____ said that my project was the most creative. The project took

weeks. _____ was worth it. The science fair was great. _____ was

more fun than I expected!

Write It

C. Answer the questions about a creative project you completed. Use subject pronouns.

10. What was the project you made? _____ made a _____.

11. Who gave you ideas about how to be creative? _____ gave me creative ideas.

12. How did you feel about your project? _____ felt _____

_____.

13. What did you learn from designing your project? _____

_____

D. (14–16) Write at least three sentences that tell more about your creative project. Use subject pronouns in your sentences.

_____

_____

_____

_____

Edit It

E. (17–20) Edit the article. Fix the four mistakes in pronouns.

> Our sewing class put on a fashion show. It was very exciting. First we sketched designs and made patterns. Then, we cut and sewed our fabric. Everyone used their imaginations. She wanted the clothes to be original. Lydia won the Most Creative Design award. He designed the perfect outfit! She is in my group of friends. They are proud of her. Our principal Mr. Johannsen was there. They congratulated Lydia.

Proofreader's Marks

Change text:

She
~~It~~ won the award.

See all Proofreader's Marks on page ix.

21 What Adds Action to a Sentence?

An Action Verb

- An **action verb** tells what the subject does.
  Some action verbs tell about an action that you cannot see.
  My parents **love** classical music.
  They **listen** to classical music on the radio all day.

- Make sure the action verb agrees with its subject. Add **-s** if the subject tells about one place, one thing, or one other person.
  I **like** many types of music.
  My **cousin listens** mostly to rap music.
  My **sister likes** country music best.
  We listen to several different radio stations.

Try It

A. Complete each sentence with an action verb.

1. Hip-hop songs _____ about the dreams and hardships of urban youth.

2. Classical pieces _____ emotion through notes rather than words.

3. My neighbor _____ to jazz music.

4. I _____ pop music.

5. My friends _____ songs with meaningful lyrics.

B. Complete each sentence with the correct form of the verb in parentheses.

6. My friends and I _____ rock music to pop. **(prefer)**

7. My favorite singer _____ country songs. **(sing)**

8. Liliana _____ the lyrics of all her favorite songs. **(memorize)**

9. I _____ the slower rhythm of country music. **(like)**

C. Answer the questions about music. Check that your verbs match their subjects.

10. What types of music do you and your friends listen to? My friends and I _____

_____.

11. Why do you like this type of music? _____ this music because

_____.

12. How do you feel when you hear your favorite songs? _____

_____

13. When do you listen to music? _____

_____

14. How does music affect other activities you do? _____

_____

15. How could you convince a family member to listen to your favorite type of music?

_____

_____

D. (16–20) Write at least five sentences about your family's favorite types of music.
Use action verbs correctly in your sentences.

_____

_____

_____

_____

_____

_____

22 How Do You Know When the Action Happens?

Look at the Verb.

An **action verb** tells what the subject does. The tense of a verb tells when the action happens.

Past ← Earlier ○ —— Now ● —— Later ○ → Future

Present Tense
sing
sin**gs**

Use the **present tense** to talk about actions that happen now or that happen on a regular basis.

My family **sings** in a choir together.

We **practice** at the community center once a week.

Try It

A. Complete each sentence with the correct form of the verb in parentheses.

1. My father _____ my family to choir practice. **(drive)**

2. We _____ singing together. **(enjoy)**

3. Sometimes my brother _____ the guitar while the choir sings. **(play)**

4. My brother and I _____ to perform for large audiences. **(like)**

5. Our choir _____ several times each month. **(perform)**

B. (6–11) Complete each sentence with a verb from the box.

believes	feel	play	practice	takes	values

My family _____ that everyone should develop musical skills. My

brother _____ guitar lessons. I _____ playing the drums.

My sister and father _____ the piano. We all _____ that

music is an important part of life. Our family _____ music.

C. Answer the questions about musical talents. Use present tense verbs in your answers.

12. What musical skills have you or your family learned through lessons and practice?

Through lessons and practice, _____.

13. How has learning about music benefited you? I have benefited because _____

_____.

14. In what other ways have you learned about music? _____

15. Would you recommend learning to play an instrument or taking singing lessons? _____

_____

16. Whose musical abilities do you admire? _____

17. How do you think developing musical talent affected this person? _____

_____

D. (18–20) Write at least three sentences about your experience learning about a certain style of music. Use present tense verbs correctly.

_____

_____

_____

E. (21–25) Edit the music review. Fix the five mistakes in present tense verb form.

Music Review

The family band called The Three of Us performs amazing shows. They shines on stage together. Ricardo play keyboard. His sister Marta sings and play guitar. Their uncle Daniel plays drums and sings, too. The family members writes and play their own music. They travel from city to city across the country. Audiences all over loves to see their shows.

Proofreader's Marks

Delete:

Greg and Suri raps̷ well.

Add text:
                    s
He play the violin.
         ^

See all Proofreader's Marks on page ix.

23 Which Action Verbs End in -s?

The Ones That Go with He, She, or It

- An **action verb** in the **present tense** tells about something that happens now or on a regular basis.

- Add **-s** to the action verb if the subject tells about one place, one thing, or one other person.

  Tina listen**s** to music when she exercises. The music give**s** her energy.

  Sean keep**s** the radio on while driving. He turn**s** the volume low to be safe.

- If the verb ends in **sh**, **ch**, **ss**, **s**, **z**, or **x**, add **-es**.

  Sharese **relaxes** when she listens to songs with a slow rhythm.

  My family **teaches** me about music.

- Do not add **-s** to the action verb if the subject is **I**, **you**, **we**, **they**, or a plural noun.

  I **watch** my family. You could **learn** from them.

  The musicians **experiment** with different styles. They **get** feedback from the audience.

Try It

A. Complete each sentence about music. Write the correct form of the verb.

1. Music _____ people's emotions and thoughts differently.
   affect / affects

2. It _____ people in various ways.
   help / helps

3. People in my family _____ to music in different ways.
   react / reacts

4. My sister _____ music videos to understand the messages of songs
   watch / watches
   more clearly.

5. When my brother wakes up to his favorite song, he energetically _____
   out of bed.
   spring / springs

6. My aunt _____ her high school friends when she hears certain songs.
   miss / misses

B. Complete each sentence with the correct form of the verb in parentheses.

7. I learn when I see how music _____ other people. **(influence)**

8. My baby cousin _____ asleep to soft music. **(fall)**

9. Now, when I have trouble going to sleep, I _____ to music with a slow rhythm, too. **(listen)**

10. My brother _____ listening to music when he does his homework. I tried turning off my MP3 player while working, and it helps me focus. **(stop)**

11. My sister _____ her favorite music videos at the end of a hard day. She says they put her in a better mood. **(watch)**

Write It

C. Answer the questions about what you have learned about how people react to music. Use action verbs.

12. How do your friends react to upbeat music? My friends _____

_____.

13. What have you learned by watching friends about how people react to music? I learned

_____.

14. Describe how you react to music in different situations. _____

_____

15. In what situations does listening to music seem more or less helpful? _____

_____

D. (16–20) Write at least five more sentences about how people react to your favorite style of music. Use action verbs correctly in your sentences.

_____

_____

_____

_____

_____

24 What Kinds of Verbs Are Can, Could, May, and Might?

They Are Helping Verbs.

- An action verb can have two parts: a **helping verb** and a **main verb**. The main verb shows the action.

  I **play** drums. I **can play** drums.

- Some helping verbs change the meaning of the action verb.

  1. Use **can** or **could** to tell about an ability.

     Yesenia **can play** the guitar well. She **could teach** guitar lessons.

  2. Use **may**, **might**, or **could** to tell about a possibility.

     Raoul **may** learn to play the keyboards. He **might like** it. He **could begin** today.

- **Can, could, may,** and **might** stay the same with all subjects. Do not add **-s**.

  Oleg **plays** the saxophone. He **can help** other people learn. He **may suggest** that you learn.

Try It

A. Complete each sentence with **can, could, may,** or **might**.

1. Anna plays the guitar. She said she _____ teach me, too.

2. I never considered playing the guitar, but Anna thinks I _____ like it.

3. Anna _____ teach me to play one song tomorrow after school.

4. If I don't like playing the guitar, I _____ try to play a few different instruments.

B. (5–8) Read each sentence. Write whether it shows an ability or possibility. Then complete the sentences with the correct helping verb.

My friend Pavel plays drums. He **(might / can)** _____ win a contest next week. Pavel said that anyone **(might / can)** _____ learn to play drums. He **(may / can)** _____ teach me a few rhythms if we have time. Maybe I **(could / can)** _____ learn to play drums, too.

C. Answer the questions about a person who has encouraged you to explore your musical interests. Use **can**, **could**, **may**, and **might** in your responses.

9. Who encouraged you to explore musical interests or abilities? _____ told me

_____.

10. What other musical abilities or interests might you explore? In the future, _____

_____.

11. Why might you explore those interests? _____

_____

12. What possibilities could learning music open for you? _____

_____

13. Can anyone develop musical talent? Why or why not? _____

_____

D. (14–16) Write at least three sentences about a creative talent you encouraged someone else to explore. Use **can**, **could**, **may**, and **might**.

_____

_____

_____

Edit It

E. (17–20) Edit the letter. Fix the four mistakes with helping verbs.

Dear Selma,

Thank you for giving me the idea to take voice lessons! I didn't think I could sing. I am surprised at the notes my voice may hit. Now I miht take more lessons. If so, I sing may in the school musical at the end of the year. Who knew that one suggestion coud make such a difference!

Sincerely,

Paula

Proofreader's Marks

Change text:
You ~~might~~ ^{can} sing a wide range of notes.

Transpose words:
We play might in a band.

See all Proofreader's Marks on page ix.

25 Use Action Verbs in the Present Tense

Remember: A verb must agree with its subject.

- Some subjects take **-s** on the action verb.

I **play** songs.	He **plays** a song.
You **sing** along.	She **sings** along.
We **sound** great.	It **sounds** great.
They **clap** loudly.	A woman **claps** loudly.

- **These verbs don't change. Do you know why?**
  We **may play** for a group of senior citizens tomorrow.
  Our music **can help** them socialize and relax together.
  They **might ask** us to come again. It **could be** a regular gig.

Try It

A. Complete each sentence with the correct form of the verb.

1. My friend and I _____ songs together.
   write / writes

2. We _____ the music at the elementary school.
   perform / performs

3. It _____ the kids a time to relax and have fun.
   give / gives

4. They _____ while we play.
   smile / smiles

5. Our music _____ a difference to them.
   make / makes

B. Draw lines to logically connect the words in the first column with those in the second column.

6. My friend Suzy	might audition.
7. Her band	may record an album.
8. I'm a drummer, so I	sings for a band.
9. The band members	could sell quickly.
10. The band's CD	needs a new drummer.

C. Answer the questions about a way you or someone you know has used music to help others. Check that your verb forms match their subjects.

11. How did you or someone you know help others through music? Using music, _____

_____.

12. Why might music be helpful to this group of people? This _____ be helpful

because _____.

13. Why did you or this person want to help this group of people? _____

_____

14. Would you recommend that others get help through music? Why? _____

_____

D. (15–16) Write at least two sentences about another way you might help someone through music. Use present tense verbs correctly.

_____

_____

_____

Edit It

E. (17–20) Edit the article. Fix the four mistakes.

A local hip-hop band helps groups in the community. The group visit the local senior citizen's center every Saturday. The guys might dance as well as they sing, and they loves performing for audiences of all ages. If they can fit it into their schedule, they can perform for the local high school during the homecoming game this fall.

Proofreader's Marks

Delete:

Most people likes music.

Add text:
                    s
He help them through music.
              ^

Change text:
           can
He may sing well.
      ^

See all Proofreader's Marks on page ix.

26 What Forms of *Be* Are Used in the Present?

Am, *Is*, and *Are*

- Use the form of the verb **be** that matches the subject.

    I **am** talented at dancing.

    You **are** good at speaking in front of audiences.

    My friend Anna **is** an excellent gymnast.

    We **are** all skilled at different activities.

    My grandparents **are** both great at singing.

    You both **are** wonderful writers.

Present Tense Forms of *Be*
I **am**
he, she, or it **is**
we, you, or they **are**

- Use **not** after the verbs **am**, **is**, and **are** to make a sentence negative. The short form of **is not** is **isn't**. The short form of **are not** is **aren't**.

    1. He **is** **not** an actor.

        He **isn't** an actor.

    2. They **are** **not** musicians.

        They **aren't** musicians.

Try It

A. Write the correct form of the verb to complete the sentence.

1–2. My mother _____ an excellent writer. She _____
  is / are   isn't / isn't
very good at spelling, but she checks her work carefully.

3. I _____ good at telling jokes. My jokes make people laugh.
  am / are

4–5. You _____ a great speaker. Other students _____
  is / are   are / aren't
as calm as you are in front of large groups.

B. (6–11) Write the correct form of **be**.

My friends and I _____ talented at different things. I _____

a good dancer. Mark _____ as good at dancing, but he is excellent at drawing.

Belinda and Tyrone _____ great musicians. Belinda _____ an expert

piano player, and Tyrone _____ an amazing guitar player.

C. Answer the questions about creative skills and talents. Use correct forms of **be** in your answers.

12. Whose talent do you admire? I admire _____ because _____.

13. Describe what makes you creative. I _____ creative because _____.

14. What creative skill or talent would you like to develop? _____

15. How is being creative helpful to you? _____

D. (16–19) Write at least four sentences about a musician or musical group you admire. Use correct forms of the verb **be**.

_____

_____

_____

_____

E. (20–25) Edit the journal entry. Fix the six mistakes with forms of the verb **be**.

Proofreader's Marks
Change text:
is
My friend ~~are~~ an artist.
See all Proofreader's Marks on page ix.

April 5

Each month the students in my class are required to give presentations. Today it's my turn again. I know that I are good at public speaking. I are an interesting speaker, and I always include some humor. Everyone laughs. Some students isn't comfortable speaking in front of the class. Sometimes I are nervous, too, but not today. My classmates is amazed at my skill. My teacher, Mr. Cafferty, are proud of my ability.

27 How Do You Show That an Action Is in Process?

Use *Am*, *Is*, or *Are* plus the *-ing* Form of the Verb.

- The **present progressive** form of the verb ends in **-ing**.
- Use **am**, **is**, or **are** plus a **main verb** with **-ing** to show that an action is in the process of happening.
  The **helping verb** must agree with the subject.
  I **am writing** a new poem.
  The poem **is taking** a long time to write.
  My friends **are asking** to read it.
  They **are waiting** patiently to read the new poem.

Try It

A. Write the correct form of the present progressive to complete each sentence.

1. My friends and I _____ a band.
        is forming / are forming

2. I _____ percussion.
        am playing / are playing

3. Jorge and Delilah _____ the vocals.
        is singing / are singing

4. We _____ after school today.
        is practicing / are practicing

5. The band _____ a variety of music.
        is performing / are performing

B. Draw lines to logically connect the words in the first column with those in the second column.

6. My classmates and I   am taking photographs of places in our city and school.

7. We   are forming a photography club.

8. I   is teaching us about our view of the world around us.

9. DeShaun   are planning to have an exhibit next month.

10. This project   is taking photos of his friends and family.

C. Answer the questions about a creative project that is teaching you about yourself or others. Use the present progressive in your responses.

11. What creative project are you working on now? I am _____
_____.

12. Who is helping you with the project? _____ me on my project.

13. What activities are others doing as part of the project? _____
_____

14. What are you learning about your own skills and talents? _____
_____

15. What is the project teaching you about working with others? _____
_____

D. (16–19) Write at least four sentences about any project you are currently involved in and what you are learning from it. Use the present progressive in your responses.

_____

_____

_____

_____

_____

Edit It

E. (20–25) Edit the radio commentary. Fix the six mistakes with the present progressive form.

Liam is describing the scene here at Fairview High for our radio listeners:

"A young man are standing on a ladder in the cafeteria. A female student is put tape around the windows. A group of students are carry boxes. What are they do? They painting a mural! We is waiting anxiously to see it when it's done."

Proofreader's Marks

Add text:
We are paint the gym.
     (ing)

Change text:
    (are)
We is working hard.

See all Proofreader's Marks on page ix.

28 What Forms of *Have* Are Used in the Present?

Have and Has

Use the form of the verb **have** that matches the subject.

- I **have** a poem for the school literary magazine.
- He **has** an illustration.
- Our school **has** a literary arts club.
- We **have** talented students in our school.
- You **have** great writing talent, too.
- They **have** excellent drawing, writing, and advertising skills.

Present Tense Forms of *Have*

I **have**

he, she, or it **has**

we, you, or they **have**

Try It

A. Complete each sentence with have or has.

1. Our school _____ a literary magazine.

2. The magazine _____ a poetry section.

3. I _____ a poem I might submit.

4. Do you _____ a piece of writing that you would like to publish?

5. Lucinda _____ a new story published in each issue.

B. Rewrite the sentences. Replace the underlined words with have or has.

6. My favorite song <u>contains</u> beautiful words. _____

7. Song lyrics <u>possess</u> the same traits as poetry, such as rhyme and alliteration. _____

_____

8. I <u>wrote</u> a few poems that would make perfect song lyrics. _____

_____

C. Answer the questions about creative writing. Use **have** or **has** as needed.

9. What types of writing do you have experience with? I _____ experience writing

_____.

10. What creative writing journals or magazines does your school have? My school _____

_____

_____.

11. Why do you think your school has these publications? _____

_____

D. (12-15) Write at least four sentences about your own creative writing using **have** or **has**.

_____

_____

_____

_____

_____

E. (16-20) Edit the introduction. Fix the five mistakes with **have** and **has**.

Introduction to This Issue

This edition of our literary magazine has two poems. Some students think that poems always words that rhyme at the end of each line. Some poems has rhythm, but not rhyme. One poem in this edition have words that rhyme. Another have a conversational style without any rhythm or rhyme. The words hav meaning and a touching message. Read on, and enjoy the words of your fellow students!

Proofreader's Marks

Add text:
has
This poem ⌃ rhythm.

Change text:
has
My poem ~~have~~ ⌃ rhyme.

See all Proofreader's Marks on page ix.

29 **What Forms of *Do* Are Used in the Present?**

Do and *Does*

• Use the form of **do** that matches the subject. You can use **do** as a **main verb** or as a **helping verb**.

I **do** my best at each audition.

My mother **does** different things to help me.

We **do hope** I can star in a musical one day.

During rehearsal, we **do** every scene many times.

The cast and crew **do** try their best to make the show a hit.

Present Tense Forms of *Do*
I **do**
he, she, or it **does**
we, you, or they **do**

• The short form of **does not** is **doesn't**. The short form of **do not** is **don't**.

1. He **does not** sing well.

   He **doesn't** sing well.

2. We **do not** want to miss the audition.

   We **don't** want to miss the audition.

Try It

A. Write the correct form of the verb to complete each sentence.

1. I _____ auditions for musicals about once a month.
   do / does

2. The directors _____ intimidate me sometimes.
   do / does

3. It _____ stop me from trying.
   don't / doesn't

4. I _____ not have a song prepared for my audition tomorrow.
   do / does

5. My friend is also auditioning. We _____ hope that we both get a part.
   do / does

6. We still _____ know where the theater is, but we will find out tonight.
   does not / don't

7. My mother will drive us to the theater. She _____ so much to help us audition.
   do / does

B. Choose words from each column to write five statements. You may use words more than once.

One thing I		every year is help with the school play.
Thierry and I always	does	the costumes and props.
But this year I	do	want to sew or build things.
This time, I will	don't	my best to get a small acting part.
Thierry		want to act in the play, too.

8. _____

9. _____

10. _____

11. _____

12. _____

Write It

C. Answer the questions about performing. Use **do**, **don't**, **does**, or **doesn't** as needed in your responses.

13. What type of performing do you do? I _____.

14. How do you prepare for a performance? To prepare, I _____
_____

15. Why do people do auditions? _____

16. What do people do at auditions? _____

D. (17–20) Write at least four sentences about what you like or don't like about performing for an audience. Use forms of **do** and **do not** in your responses.

_____

_____

_____

_____

_____

30 Use Verbs to Talk About the Present

Remember: The verbs **be**, **have**, and **do** each have more than one form in the present. Use the form that goes with the subject.

Forms of *Be*	Forms of *Have*	Forms of *Do*
I **am**	I **have**	I **do**
he, she, or it **is**	he, she, or it **has**	he, she, or it **does**
we, you, or they **are**	we, you, or they **have**	we, you, or they **do**

Try It

A. Complete the sentences with the correct present tense form of the verb in parentheses.

1. Our classmates _____ enthusiastic about literary arts. **(be)**

2. I _____ the editor of our school magazine. **(be)**

3. Diego _____ the proofreading for the magazine. **(do)**

4. I _____ respect for anyone who writes poems. **(have)**

5. This year the school _____ a group of students who are putting together a poetry slam. **(have)**

6. They _____ poets who have participated in poetry slams. **(be)**

7. During the poetry slam, each poet _____ a turn on stage. **(have)**

8. The students _____ the decorations for the event. **(do)**

9. We _____ so excited about hearing our schoolmates do poetry slams on stage! **(be)**

10. We _____ hope the slam is a success **(do)**

B. (11–16) Read the interview. Write the correct verb to complete the sentence.

Q. Why do you do poetry slams?

A. I _____ a lot of encouragement for my poetry. My brother and I
               have / has
enter poetry slams together on the weekends. My brother _____
                                                     have / has
a part-time job, so I _____ more preparing for the contests than
                    do / does
he does. He _____ a lot of fun doing slams anyway.
             have / has
They _____ a good way to develop our talent with poetry
        are / am
and rhythm. We _____ more confident because of this hobby.
          is / are

Write It

C. Answer the questions about your experience with poetry or events like poetry slams. Use forms of **be**, **have**, and **do**.

17. Are poetry slams more popular than poetry readings? _____

_____

18. When have you read, written, or spoken poetry? _____

_____

19. What are your feelings and thoughts about poetry? _____

_____

20. Who is your favorite poet? What is your favorite poem? _____

_____

D. (21–25) Write at least five more sentences that describe your experience with poetry. Use the correct forms of **be**, **have**, and **do**.

_____

_____

_____

_____

_____

_____

✔ Capitalize the Names of Groups

- The names of some groups are proper nouns and should be capitalized. A **proper noun** is a noun that names a specific person, place, or thing. These include institutions, businesses, organizations, and government agencies.

   Institution: Newberry Public Library

   Business: Fig Media Incorporated

   Organization: National High School Association

- The names of nonspecific groups should not be capitalized.

   a library

   a company

   an association

Try It

A. Use proofreader's marks to correct the capitalization error in each sentence.

1. Our school uniforms are made at American Uniform association. It is one of the largest uniform Companies in the country.

2. Our school is the only school in district 12 that requires school uniforms. The other districts do not have a school uniform policy.

Proofreader's Marks

Capitalize:
   I work at edge hair salon.

Do not capitalize:
   I work at a Hair Salon.

See all Proofreader's Marks on page ix.

B. (3–10) Edit the letter. Fix the eight mistakes in capitalization.

Dear Ms. Gomez:

As a Member of the Student Council, I do not think our school should require students to wear uniforms. Other Districts do not require students to wear uniforms. In fact, district 16 has issued school dress codes to solve the clothing problem. We propose that a dress code, not a uniform policy, be issued for Glendale High school.

Sincerely,

Yvonne Gustin

Vice President, Glendale high school Student Council

✓ Use Colons Correctly

- Use a **colon** after a complete sentence to set off a list of items, an explanation, or a quotation.

    You must wear the new school uniform: long pants or a skirt below the knee, a shirt with a collar, and a pair of loafers.

    The new rule is simple: You must wear the uniform whenever you are at school.

    Remember the dress code's guiding principle: "Our dress reflects the pride we take in ourselves and the value we place on our education."

- Capitalize the first word after a colon if it is a **proper noun** or the first word of a complete sentence.

    Three students helped write the dress code rules: **Anika**, Tom, and Sam.

    They added the following rule: **Students** must also follow the dress code during school-sponsored outings.

Try It

A. For each sentence, add a colon or capitalize a word.

11. Our high school has a new dress code: students cannot wear clothing that is inappropriate or offensive.

12. Students are not allowed to wear baseball caps, tank tops, shorts, or T-shirts with words or pictures.

13. Our school handbook lists one exception "On half days, students may wear jeans and non-offensive T-shirts."

Proofreader's Marks
Add a colon:
These students have already bought their uniforms⌄ Valerie, Sam, and Angel.
Capitalize:
There's a new rule: you can't wear flip-flops.

B. (14–15) Write two sentences that contain a list of reasons why you do or do not want to wear a school uniform. One sentence should have a colon; the other should not.

_____

_____

_____

Edit and Proofread

✓ Check Your Spelling

Homonyms are words that sound alike but have different meanings and spellings. Spell these homonyms correctly when you proofread.

Homonyms and Their Meanings	**Examples**
to (preposition) = toward	Tiana went **to** a new school.
two (adjective) = the number 2	The book has **two** parts.
too (adverb) = also, more than enough	The rule is **too** strict.
your (adjective) = belonging to you	**Your** report was interesting.
you're (contraction) = you are	**You're** the first person in line.

Try It

A. Complete each sentence about school uniforms. Use the correct homonym.

16. Unfortunately, the company charges _____*too*_____ much
    for the uniforms.
    to / two / too

17. How can you afford _____*your*_____ uniform at those prices?
    your / you're

18. You have to buy your own socks, _____*too*_____.
    to / two / too

19. The worst thing about wearing a school uniform is that you lose

    _____*your*_____ freedom of expression.
    your / you're

20. Clothes and jewelry allow us _____*to*_____ be creative.
    to / two / too

B. (21–23) Do you think schools should issue a uniform policy, create a dress code, or allow students to wear whatever they want to wear? Write at least three sentences. Be sure to use one homonym in each sentence.

I think that the idea of using uniforms is too bad.
I do not like to use uniforms. I went to two schools
where you had to use uniforms.

✓ Use Correct Verb Forms in the Present Tense

- **Have, be,** and **do** are irregular verbs. They have more different forms in their present tense than regular verbs do.

    I **have** a dress code at school. She has one, too.

    Are you satisfied with the decision? **Is** your friend satisfied? I definitely **am**.

    I **do** own a uniform. So **does** he.

- Use **not** after each form of **be** or **do** to make a sentence negative.

    She **is not** happy. She **does not** want to wear a uniform.

Forms of *Have*
I, we, you, or they **have**
he, she, or it **has**

Forms of *Be*
I **am**
he, she, or it **is**
we, you, or they **are**

Forms of *Do*
I, we, you, or they **do**
he, she, or it **does**

Try It

A. (24–28) Edit the paragraph. Fix the five verbs that do not match their subjects.

<u>High School Dress Code Policy</u>: Students is to follow the dress code at all times. If they doesn't wear the proper attire, then they aren't following the dress code. No student have permission to disobey the code. There is no exceptions to the rule. The dress code are a necessary part of a positive learning environment for students.

Proofreader's Marks

Delete:

I like your new ~~new~~ uniform.

Add text:
did
Where you buy your uniform?

B. (29–30) Write at least two sentences telling how students, teachers, and parents might feel about the dress code policy. Use a form of the verb **have, be,** or **do** in each sentence.

That students have to wear whatever they feel comfortable with.

They do not have to follow the dress code.

31 How Do You Show That an Action Already Happened?

Add -ed to the Verb.

- Action in the **present tense** happens now or on a regular basis.
- Action in the **past tense** happened earlier.

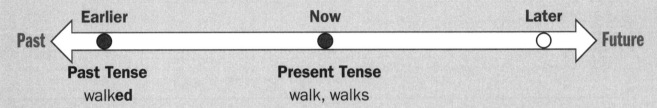

Past ⟵ **Earlier** ● ──── **Now** ● ──── **Later** ○ ⟶ **Future**

Past Tense
walk**ed**

Present Tense
walk, walks

Add **-ed** to most verbs when you talk about a past action. If there is more than one verb in a sentence, they must all be in the same tense.

1. Today, Tomás **walks** home from work.

Yesterday, Tomás **walked** home, too.

2. Today, he **smells** smoke, **looks** around, then **picks up** his pace.

Yesterday, he **smelled** smoke, **looked** around, then **picked up** his pace.

Try It

A. Complete each sentence with the past tense of the verb in parentheses.

1. Tomás _____ the corner and saw a house on fire. **(pass)**

2. A woman _____ that her child was inside. **(scream)**

3. Tomás _____ the house, searched the rooms, and listened. **(enter)**

4. "Help me!" _____ a voice. **(yell)**

B. (5–8) Complete each sentence with a past tense.

Tomás _____ for the child. He _____ to see a little boy.

Tomás _____ up the boy. He _____ outside with the child.

C. Answer the questions about Tomás's story. Use the past tense.

   9. What did Tomás do that was brave? He _____

_____.

  10. What was it like inside the burning house? Smoke _____

_____.

  11. Would you have done something different than what Tomás did? Write about it using the

     past tense. _____

_____

D. (12–14) Think about a time when you or someone you know was brave.
Write at least three sentences telling what happened. Use the past tense.
Use three verbs in one of your sentences.

_____

_____

_____

_____

_____

Edit It

E. (15–20) Edit the journal entry. Fix six mistakes with verbs.

August 10

Yesterday, it rained all day. The streets filled
with water, and soon the river flooded. When
the water reaches the front door, we climb
onto the roof. We watch as many things
float by. Some men in a boat help us escape.
We thank them many times.

Proofreader's Marks

Change text:

    sighed
They sigh when it was
over. ∧

See all Proofreader's Marks
on page ix.

32 Can You Just Add *-ed* to Form a Verb in the Past?

Not Always

> Most verbs end with **-ed** to show the past tense. Sometimes you have to change the spelling of the verb before you add **-ed**.
>
> **1.** If a verb ends in silent **e**, drop the **e**. Then add **-ed**.
>
> My grandmother liv**ed** in a small village when she was younger. **(live)**
> The people in the village relat**ed** this story for many years. **(relate)**
>
> **2.** Some one-syllable verbs end in one vowel and one consonant. Double the consonant before you add **-ed**.
>
> There were men who robb**ed** villages. **(rob)**
> The story tells how a girl stopp**ed** these robbers. **(stop)**

Try It

A. Complete each sentence with the past tense of the verb in parentheses.

1. One day, at home alone, the girl _____ some strangers coming. **(notice)**

2. She _____ they were robbers. **(believe)**

3. The girl _____ how to stop them. **(plan)**

4. She _____ a white cloth. **(grab)**

5. Then she _____ outside. **(race)**

6. The robbers saw the house was empty and _____. **(stay)**

B. (7–11) Complete each sentence with a past tense verb.

At dusk, the girl _____ behind the house. She _____ on the walls and moans. She _____ the white cloth like it was a ghost. She _____ the robbers so much that they left the village. The villagers _____ the girl Clever One.

Write It

C. Answer the questions. Use the past tense.

12. What do you think the robbers did when they thought they saw a ghost? They _____

_____.

13. What do you think the girl did after the robbers left? She _____

_____.

D. (14–17) Think about a story you have heard about a hero or legend. Write at least four sentences telling the main events in the story. Use the past tense.

_____

_____

_____

_____

_____

Edit It

E. (18–25) Edit the journal entry. Fix eight mistakes with verbs.

January 14

Last week, it snowed so much that no one dares go out. We use up all our food, so Father decides to go to town. Ice covers the roads. The horse slips on the ice, so Father walks many miles to the store. Then he drags a box of food back to us through the snow. Finally, he open the door.

Proofreader's Marks

Change text:

We ~~close~~ closed the door after Father.

See all Proofreader's Marks on page ix.

33 When Do You Use *Was* and *Were*?

When You Tell About the Past

The verb **be** has special forms to tell about the present and the past.

Earlier	Now	Later
Past ←		→ Future

Past Tense	Present Tense
I **was**	I **am**
you **were**	you **are**
he, she, or it **was**	he, she, or it **is**
we **were**	we **are**
they **were**	they **are**

Present: Our school's soccer team **is** not very good.

   Past: Last year, it **was** the worst team in the league.

Present: Our athletes **are** always surprised when they do well.

   Past: They **were** really surprised when Felipe scored the winning goal.

Try It

A. Rewrite each sentence using the past tense of the <u>verb</u>.

1. It <u>is</u> our first game of the season. _____

2. We <u>are</u> behind. _____

3. There <u>are</u> only two minutes left. _____

4. Felipe <u>is</u> in the middle of the field when he got the ball. _____

_____

5. His teammates <u>are</u> excited and yelled for him to pass it. _____

_____

B. (6–13) Complete each sentence with the correct form of the past tense of be.

Felipe _____ small but quick. Two guys from the other team

_____ in his way. Felipe kicked the ball and leaped between them. It

looked like he _____ in the air! When he landed, he _____

able to kick the ball into the goal. All the fans _____ excited because

the teams had tied. At the kick-off, Felipe _____ the first to get the

ball. We _____ amazed to see him dribble it and score again. It

_____ unbelievable!

Write It

C. Answer the questions. Use was and were in your answers.

14. Write about your response to Felipe's part in the soccer game. _____

_____

15. How might people exaggerate what Felipe did in the game? _____

_____

16. Why might people want to exaggerate? _____

_____

D. (17–20) Think about someone you know who did something amazing. Write at least four sentences telling what happened. Use was and were.

_____

_____

_____

_____

_____

34 When Do You Use *Had*?

When You Tell About the Past

The verb **have** uses special forms to show the present and the past.

Earlier	Now	Later

Past ← ——●——————————●——————————○——→ Future

Past Tense	Present Tense
I **had**	I **have**
you **had**	you **have**
he, she, or it **had**	he, she, or it **has**
we **had**	we **have**
they **had**	they **have**

Present: We **have** a new teacher.

Past: We **had** a new teacher.

Present: She **has** a book about World War II.

Past: She **had** a book about World War II.

Try It

A. Rewrite each sentence, changing the <u>verb</u> to the past tense.

1. The book <u>has</u> many interesting stories. _____

2. It <u>has</u> photos of real heroes. _____

3. They <u>have</u> frightening experiences. _____

4. One family <u>has</u> a difficult decision to make. _____

_____

5. They <u>have</u> friends who were in great danger. _____

_____

B. (6–14) Complete each sentence with the past tense of have.

The family _____ a place for their friends to hide. Their friends

_____ nowhere else to go. The family _____ to keep the

hiding place a secret or they would be in danger, too. The family _____

to bring food and water to their hidden friends. The friends _____ to be

silent so no one would find them. But they _____ a little boy. One day,

he _____ a fever. The family _____ to find a doctor who

could be trusted. Luckily, the people in hiding survived. When the war ended, they

_____ a celebration to thank the family for saving their lives.

Write It

C. Answer the questions. Use the past tense of have in your answers.

15. Why were the people in the family heroes? The family _____

_____.

16. What do you think the people in hiding said about the family after the war? They _____

_____.

D. (17–20) Think about a person or group that acted heroically in the past. Write at least four sentences telling what they did. Use the past tense of have in your answers.

_____

_____

_____

_____

_____

_____

35 Use Verb Tenses

Remember: You have to change the verb to show the past tense.
Be sure to use the same tense for all verbs in the same sentence.

Add **-ed** to most verbs. You may need to make a spelling change before you add **-ed**.

Present Tense	Past Tense
work, works	worked
want, wants	wanted
drag, drags	dragged
live, lives	lived

Use special forms for the past tense of **be** and **have**.

Forms of *Be*	
Present Tense	Past Tense
am, is, are	was, were

Forms of *Have*	
Present Tense	Past Tense
have, has	had

Try It

A. Complete each sentence with the correct form of the verb.

1. Last year, I _____ an assignment to write about a hero.
   <u>have / had</u>

2. I _____ topics and _____ to research Cesar
   <u>consider / considered</u>   <u>decide / decided</u>
   Chavez.

3. I _____ that Cesar Chavez and his family _____
   <u>learn / learned</u>   <u>are / were</u>
   migrant farm workers.

4. Cesar Chavez _____ a union for farm workers in 1962.
   <u>start / started</u>

B. Complete each sentence with the past tense of the verb in parentheses.

5. Chavez _____ better conditions for farm workers. **(want)**

6. Some grape growers _____ to listen to the union. **(refuse)**

7. The union _____ people to boycott the grape growers. **(ask)**

Write It

C. Answer the questions. Use the past tense.

8. Cesar Chavez believed in nonviolence, even when others behaved violently. How do you think this helped the farm workers? I think _____

   _____.

9. In one sentence, tell three actions you would take to remain nonviolent. Use parallel structure. _____

   _____

   _____

10. What do you think would have happened if the union members had acted violently?

    _____

    _____

D. (11–13) What do you think about Cesar Chavez? Write at least three sentences explaining your opinion. Use the past tense in some of your sentences.

_____

_____

_____

_____

_____

Edit It

E. (14–20) Edit the paragraph. Fix seven mistakes with verbs.

When Cesar Chavez was a boy, his family moved around California. They have to go where there is work for them. Cesar pick fruits and vegetables in many places. He work very long days. He helps his family and earns money. This was the beginning of a life spent helping others. He want to help migrant farm workers.

Proofreader's Marks
Change text: worked
Cesar Chavez ~~work~~ hard. ∧
See all Proofreader's Marks on page ix.

36 How Do You Show That an Action Already Happened?

Change the Verb.

Add **-ed** to most verbs to show that an action already happened.
Use special past tense forms for **irregular verbs**.

Present	Past	Example in the Past
ring	rang	The fire alarm **rang** in the middle of the night.
bring	brought	The alarm **brought** my dad to his feet.
know	knew	Dad and the other firefighters **knew** what to do.
get	got	They **got** dressed.
find	found	They **found** their gear.
go, goes	went	Then they **went** to the fire truck.
stand	stood	Dad **stood** in the back of the truck.
see	saw	Then they **saw** the house on fire.

Try It

A. Rewrite each sentence changing the <u>verb</u> to the past tense.

1. The firefighters <u>know</u> what to do. _____

2. They <u>have</u> little time to do it. _____

3. They <u>get</u> out the hoses. _____

4. Some of the firefighters <u>stand</u> with the hoses outside the house. _____

_____

5. Then they <u>see</u> a man who said there was someone inside. _____

_____

B. Complete each sentence with the past tense of the verb in parentheses.

6. Dad _____ a mask to help with breathing. **(get)**

7. Then he _____ into the building. **(go)**

8. He _____ he had to hurry. **(know)**

9. He _____ a man inside. **(find)**

10. Dad _____ the man out. **(bring)**

Write It

C. Answer the questions. Use some irregular verbs in the past tense.

11. How did Dad find the man in the building? He _____

_____.

12. What did the firefighters do that was heroic? They _____

_____.

D. (13–16) Think about someone in your community whose job required him
or her to be brave. Write at least four sentences telling what this person did
that was heroic. Use the past tense of some irregular verbs.

_____

_____

_____

_____

_____

Edit It

E. (17–20) Edit the news report. Fix four mistakes.

Yesterday, there was an accident. A truck goes off the road.
They find the driver asleep at the wheel. Paramedics come and
treated the driver. Then they bringed him to the hospital.

Proofreader's Marks

Change text:
                came
They ~~come~~ in time to
help. ^

See all Proofreader's Marks
on page ix.

37 How Do You Show That an Action Already Happened?

Change the Verb.

Add **-ed** to most verbs to show that an action already happened.
Use special past tense forms for **irregular verbs**.

Present	Past	Example in the Past
take	took	My grandmother **took** me under her wing.
read	read	She **read** me stories about people who were kind.
say	said	She **said** kind people could be heroes.
tell	told	She **told** me that I could be a hero, too.
make	made	Her words **made** a big impression on me.
feel	felt	I **felt** like helping others.
speak	spoke	I was glad she **spoke** to me like that.
keep	kept	I always **kept** her words in mind.

Try It

A. Complete each sentence with the past tense of the verb in parentheses.

1. My grandmother _____ me some money for my birthday. **(give)**

2. I _____ the money for a while. **(keep)**

3. Then I _____ what to buy. **(know)**

4. On my way to the store, I _____ a homeless man. **(see)**

5. He _____ with a sign asking for food. **(stand)**

B. Rewrite each sentence, changing the <u>verb</u> to the past tense.

6. I <u>hide</u> my money at first. _____

_____

7. Then, I <u>feel</u> bad. _____

_____

8. I <u>take</u> some sandwiches to the man. _____

_____

9. He <u>tells</u> me he had not eaten for two days. _____

_____

10. He <u>says</u> I saved his life. _____

_____

Write It

C. Answer the questions. Use the past tense of some irregular verbs.

11. Do you think the narrator acted heroically? Why or why not? I think _____

_____.

12. What do you think the homeless man did after the narrator gave him food? He _____

_____.

D. (13–15) Think about a time that you did a small act that made a big difference. Write at least three sentences telling what happened. Use the past tense of some irregular verbs.

_____

_____

_____

_____

_____

㊳ How Do You Show That an Action Was In Process?

Use *Was* or *Were* Plus the *-ing* Form of the Verb.

- Sometimes you want to show that an action was happening over a period of time in the past. Use the past progressive form of the verb.

- To form the past progressive, use the helping verb **was** or **were** plus a main verb that ends in **-ing**. The **helping verb** must agree with the subject.

  Shawna **was planning** to enter the dance competition.
  I **was helping** her with her moves.
  Some other girls **were teasing** Shawna.
  They **were saying** she was not a good dancer.
  Everyone **was thinking** these girls would win.

Try It

A. Complete each sentence with the past progressive form of the verb in parentheses.

1. Shawna _____ badly. **(feel)**

2. She _____ that the girls were right. **(think)**

3. "I _____ my steps," she said. **(forget)**

4. "Those girls _____ me." **(watch)**

5. "I know they _____ at me." **(laugh)**

6. I said, "They _____ to lower your confidence." **(try)**

7. "They _____ that you would drop out." **(hope)**

8. I _____ Shawna that she was a good dancer. **(tell)**

9. Finally, Shawna _____ to me. **(listen)**

10. At the competition, she _____ when she went onstage. **(smile)**

B. Rewrite each sentence using the past progressive of the <u>verb</u>.

11. My brother <u>worries</u> about his math test. _____

_____

12. He <u>studies</u> all night. _____

_____

13. His friends <u>make</u> fun of him. _____

_____

14. I <u>encourage</u> him not to give up. _____

_____

15. I <u>help</u> him study the night before the test. _____

_____

Write It

C. Answer the questions. Use the past progressive tense of verbs in your answers.

16. What do you think happened to Shawna during the dance competition? Shawna _____

_____.

17. How have you encouraged a friend to do something? I _____

_____.

D. (18–20) Think about a time when someone encouraged you. Write at least three sentences telling what happened. Use the past progressive tense in some of your sentences.

_____

_____

_____

_____

_____

39 How Do You Tell About the Future?

Use *Will* Before the Verb.

The **future tense** of a verb shows that an action will happen later.

Earlier   Now   Later

Past ← —————— ○ —————— ○ —————— ● ——→ Future

Future Tense

- To form the future tense, use **will** before the main verb.
  We **will complete** safety training at work.

- Or use **am, is,** or **are** plus **going to** before the main verb.
  We **are going to complete** safety training at work.

- **If will** or **am, is,** or **are** plus **going to** comes before the first verb in a series, all three verbs are in the future-tense.
  The owner **will close** for the day, **provide** lunch, and **pay** us for the day.

Try It

A. Complete each sentence. Use the future tense of the verb in parentheses. More than one answer is possible.

1. We _____ how to stay safe in a restaurant kitchen. **(learn)**

2. The manager _____ a video about handling food safely. **(show)**

3. The head cook _____ how to put out a grease fire. **(demonstrate)**

4. We _____ the fire extinguisher and learn first-aid. **(use)**

5. We _____ a test to show what we learned. **(take)**

B. Use the future tense of a verb from the box. More than one answer is possible.

be	help	know	practice

6. Learning about safety _____ us in an emergency.

7. We _____ what to do if someone gets hurt.

8. We _____ more careful and _____ safety in the kitchen now.

C. Answer the questions. Use future tense verbs in your sentences.

9. How will taking a CPR class help a babysitter? It _____
_____.

10. How will first-aid training help people who work at the mall? They _____
_____.

11. How could someone working in an office benefit from first-aid training? _____
_____.

D. (12–16) What are your plans for learning how to act in an emergency?
Write at least five sentences telling what you will do to prepare yourself
for emergencies. Use future tense verbs. In one sentence, use three
future tense verbs.

_____

_____

_____

_____

_____

_____

Edit It

E. (17–20) Edit the class description. Use the future tense with will. Fix four
mistakes.

Basic Life Guarding 101

This class will teach water safety to people who wish to lifeguard.
Students learn the basics of water rescue. They demonstrate
their knowledge of water safety. Instructors present material
in various ways. Students have to pass a test at the end of the
class.

Proofreader's Marks

Change text:
  will help
It help me at work.
   ^

See all Proofreader's Marks
on page ix.

ⓐ Use Verb Tenses

Remember: You have to change the verb to show when an action happens. The action can happen in the **present**, **past**, or **future**.

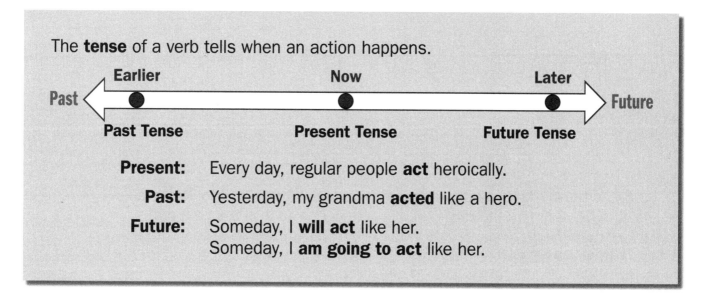

The **tense** of a verb tells when an action happens.

Earlier   Now   Later

Past ◄—————————————————————► Future

Past Tense   Present Tense   Future Tense

Present: Every day, regular people **act** heroically.

Past: Yesterday, my grandma **acted** like a hero.

Future: Someday, I **will act** like her.
Someday, I **am going to act** like her.

Try It

A. Complete each sentence. Use the correct tense of the verb in parentheses.

1. Yesterday, my grandmother _____ home. **(past progressive of drive)**

2. She _____ a car crash into a pole. **(past tense of see)**

3. The driver _____ for help. **(past progressive of call)**

4. "I _____ you," Grandma said. **(future tense of help)**

B. Complete each sentence with the correct tense of a verb from the box. More than one answer is possible.

help	know	limp	save	take

5. Grandma _____ she had to act quickly.

6. She _____ the man's arm and _____ him out of the car.

7. He _____, but he was smiling, too.

8. "You _____ my life," he told Grandma.

C. Answer the questions. Use different tenses to make your meaning clear.

9. Why did the narrator want to be like his or her grandma? The narrator _____

_____.

10. What do you think will happen to the injured driver? Use two future tense verbs in your sentence. I think _____

_____

_____.

D. (11–13) Think about an ordinary person you know who is a hero. Write at least three sentences telling what this person has done in the past and what you think he or she will do in the future. Use different tenses to make your meaning clear.

_____

_____

_____

_____

_____

E.

Rollo the Wonder Dog

Yesterday was an extraordinary day. Rollo know something was wrong. Grandpa lies on the floor. Rollo bark all morning. Finally, a neighbor comes to see what was wrong. Grandpa breathes, but he was very ill.

"You live," the neighbor tell him, "thanks to Rollo the Wonder Dog!"

Proofreader's Marks

Change text:
heard
The neighbor ~~hear~~ Rollo barking.

See all Proofreader's Marks on page ix.

41 How Do Nouns Work in a Sentence?

They Can Be the Subject or the Object.

- Nouns can be the **subject** of a sentence.

    Teens have a bad reputation.
    subject

- Nouns can also be the **object** of an action verb. To find the object, turn the verb into a question like: "Distrust whom?" Your answer is the object.

    Many adults distrust **teens**.
                    verb   object

- Many English sentences follow this pattern: **subject → verb → object**.

    Some teens cause problems.
    subject   verb   object

    But my friends helped our community.
        subject   verb   object

Try It

A. **Read each sentence. Write whether the underlined noun is a subject or an object.**

1. Many <u>parents</u> have jobs. _____

2. Their children take the <u>bus</u> home after school. _____

3. No one is able to watch these <u>kids</u>. _____

4. Some <u>kids</u> need help with homework. _____

5. Other children make <u>trouble</u>. _____

6. My <u>friends</u> started a club for kids after school. _____

7. A neighbor offered a <u>room</u>. _____

8. The grocer donated <u>snacks</u>. _____

9. The teens give <u>help</u> to the kids. _____

10. These <u>teens</u> solved a social problem. _____

B. Choose an object from the box to complete each sentence.

article	cans	example	garden
meals	principal	program	students

11. Our school has a _____ to fight hunger.

12. Some students prepare _____ for elderly people who can't cook.

13. One class distributes _____ of food.

14. The science class planted a _____ for the community.

15. A reporter wrote an _____ about our program.

16. Other schools followed our _____.

17. The mayor thanked the _____ for their work.

18. She congratulated our _____, too.

C. Answer the questions. Be sure your sentences contain a subject and an object.

19. What have you done to work for social change? I _____

_____.

20. What could the people in your community do to create social change? _____

_____

D. (21–25) What laws or situations would you like to change in your community?
Write at least five sentences telling what you would change and why. Use
subjects and objects in your sentences.

_____

_____

_____

_____

_____

_____

(42) Why Are There So Many Pronouns?

Some Work as Subjects, and Some Work as Objects.

- Use a **subject pronoun** as the subject of a sentence.

  My uncle **Steve** believes in equality. **He** fought for civil rights.
  _{subject}

  The **civil rights movement** happened in the 1960s. **It** was an important time.
  _{subject}

- Use an **object pronoun** as the object of the verb.

  Many people disliked segregation. These people fought against **it**.
  _{object}

  Steve helped to register voters. Some people distrusted **him**.
  _{object}

- The pronouns **you** and **it** stay the same as subjects and objects.

Pronouns	
Subject	Object
I	me
you	you
he	him
she	her
it	it

Try It

A. Complete each pair of sentences with a pronoun. Circle the noun from the first sentence that the pronoun refers to.

1. One man shouted at Steve. The man called _____ names.

2. Some kids tried to beat up Steve. Luckily, _____ wasn't hurt.

3. Steve talked to an elderly woman. _____ had never voted before.

4. Steve handed Mrs. Hill a form. Steve told _____ the form would let her vote.

B. (5–9) Complete the sentences with subject and object pronouns.

A newspaper published a letter to the editor. _____ said that some people shouldn't be allowed to vote. Steve read the article. _____ made _____ mad. _____ called the woman who wrote the letter. Steve told _____ that everyone had the right to vote.

C. Answer the questions. Use subject and object pronouns.

10. How did Steve make changes in our country? He _____

_____.

11. Why is voting important? It _____

_____.

12. What would you like to say to Steve? You _____

_____.

D. (13–15) Think about someone whose actions helped change history. Write at least three sentences telling what happened. Use subject and object pronouns.

_____

_____

_____

_____

_____

_____

Edit It

E. (16–20) Edit the letter. Fix five mistakes with pronouns.

Dear Steve,

 My mother asked me to thank you. Steve helped she vote. Mother told I that the first time her voted was special. He was the most important day in her life. She will never forget it. Voting is an important responsibility. Everyone who is eligible should vote!

Sincerely,

Sally Hill

Proofreader's Marks

Change text:

She
~~Her~~ wanted to thank you.

See all Proofreader's Marks on page ix.

Name _____ Date _____

43 Do You Ever Talk About Yourself?

Then Learn to Use the Words _I_ and _Me_.

Subject Pronoun: I	**Object Pronoun: me**

• Use the pronoun **I** in the **subject** of a sentence.
 	
    I like Angelo's Grocery.
 	
• In a compound subject, name yourself last.
 	
  Correct: **Tess and I** go there after school.
 	
             She and I like to buy a snack.
 	
  Incorrect: Me and Tess like Mr. Angelo.
	• Use the pronoun **me** as the **object**. Mr. and Mrs. Angelo are friendly to **me**.
	
	• In a compound object, name yourself last.
	
	  Correct: Mrs. Angelo smiles at **Tess and me**.
	
	          Mr. Angelo says hello to **her and me**.
	
	  Incorrect: Mr. Angelo gave samples to Tess and I.
	
	          He asked me and her if they were good.

Try It

A. Complete each sentence with **I** or **me**.

1. "_____ have a problem," said Mr. Angelo.

          I / me

2. Tess and _____ learned that a big grocery was moving next door.

          I / me

3. "That store will put _____ out of business," said Mr. Angelo.

          I / me

4. My friend and _____ decided to help Mr. Angelo.

          I / me

B. (5–8) Complete the sentences with **I** or **me**.

I wrote ten reasons why people should keep shopping at Angelo's Grocery.

Tess helped _____ make copies of the list. Tess and _____

posted the list around town. Some people asked Tess and _____

questions. Tess and _____ answered them.

C. Answer the questions. Use **I** and **me**.

9. What would you do if Angelo's Grocery were in your neighborhood? *If Angelo's Grocery were in my neighborhood,* _____

_____ .

10. What kinds of neighborhood businesses are important to you and your friends? _____

_____

_____

D. (11–14) Now write at least four sentences telling why a neighborhood business is important to you and what you can do to support it. Use **I** and **me** in your sentences.

_____

_____

_____

_____

_____

Edit It

E. (15–20) Edit the letter. Fix six mistakes.

Dear Mayor Roberts:

My friends and I think you should not let a big chain grocery store come to our neighborhood. Our local grocer told my friends and I that he would go out of business. Me like shopping at Angelo's Grocery. My family and me will not shop anywhere else. Thank you for listening to I. My friends and me hope you can help us. Me think we have to support our small local businesses.

Sincerely,

Greg Yee

Proofreader's Marks
Change text:
My friends and me̶
wanted to help.
See all Proofreader's Marks on page ix.

44 Which Pronouns Refer to More Than One Person?

We, You, They, and *Us, You, Them*

With so many pronouns, how do you know which one to use in a sentence?

Pronouns	
Subject	**Object**
we	us
you	you
they	them

- Use a **subject pronoun** as the subject.

  My **friends and I** use the library a lot. **We** like to study there.
  subject

  The **city council members** had a meeting. **They** want to close the library.
  subject

- Use an **object pronoun** as the object of the verb.

  People in my neighborhood were upset. Closing the library will affect **them**.
  object

  We talked to the city council members. The council members listened to **us**.
  subject   object

Try It

A. Complete each pair of sentences with a pronoun. Circle the word or words each pronoun refers to.

1. The council members explained the problem. _____ said there was
   They / Them
   not enough money to run the library.

2. The library is important to my neighbors and me. It gives _____ a
   we / us
   place to read and study.

3. "You and I can keep the library open," said my friend. "_____ can
   We / Us
   have a carwash to raise money."

4. We made signs advertising the carwash. Then we posted _____
   they / them
   around town.

5. My friends and I collected buckets and sponges. A store gave _____
   we / us
   soap.

B. (6–10) Complete the sentences using subject and object pronouns.

My brother and I stood on a corner with a sign. Lots of people driving by

saw _____. _____ drove in to the carwash. Some people

got out of their cars. Other people sat in _____. My neighbors

and I washed the cars. _____ made them shine. The people paid

_____ ten dollars per car.

Write It

C. Answer the questions. Use subject and object pronouns in your sentences.

11. What do you think the neighbors did with the money they made? I think _____

_____

_____.

12. What do you think the city council members might say to the neighbors? _____

_____

_____

D. (13–15) Think about an issue in your school or community that people are trying to change. Write at least three sentences telling how you can participate. Use subject and object pronouns.

_____

_____

_____

_____

_____

45 Use Subject and Object Pronouns

Remember: Use a subject pronoun as the subject of a sentence. Use an object pronoun as the object of the verb.

Subject Pronouns	I	you	he	she	it	we	you	they
Object Pronouns	me	you	him	her	it	us	you	them

My friends and **I** have many heroes. **We** read about **them**. Helen Keller is one of our heroes. Do you know about **her**? **She** inspired many people. Cesar Chavez is another hero. **He** helped farm workers.

Try It

A. Rewrite each sentence, replacing the underlined word or words with the correct pronoun.

1. <u>Susan B. Anthony</u> is another hero of mine. _____
   _____

2. Susan B. Anthony wanted <u>women</u> to be able to vote. _____
   _____

3. <u>Women</u> did not have the same rights as men. _____
   _____

4. Some men did not agree with <u>Susan B. Anthony</u>. _____
   _____

5. <u>My dad</u> says that Susan B. Anthony is his hero, too. _____
   _____

B. (6–10) Complete the sentences with subject or object pronouns.

My friends and _____ read about Mohandas Gandhi.

_____ think Gandhi was a great man. _____ helped

his countrymen and women overthrow British rule. Although _____

suffered a lot, Gandhi encouraged _____ to be nonviolent.

C. **Answer the questions. Use subject and object pronouns.**

11. Why do many people consider Martin Luther King, Jr. a hero? Many people _____

_____

_____.

12. How can an ordinary person be a hero? _____

_____

_____

D. **(13–16) Think about one of your heroes. Write at least four sentences telling what this person has done that inspires you. Use subject and object pronouns.**

_____

_____

_____

_____

_____

_____

Edit It

E. **(17–20) Edit the paragraph. Fix four mistakes with subject and object pronouns.**

Nelson Mandela is one of my heroes. He was born in a small village in South Africa. Him fought against unjust laws and changed they. The government sent he to jail. But Mandela continued to inspire people. Them worked with Mandela to change the laws. Mandela became South Africa's first black president in 1994.

Proofreader's Marks
Change text:
us
Mandela gave ~~we~~ hope.
See all Proofreader's Marks on page ix.

✔ Capitalize Proper Nouns

Capitalize specific days of the week and the names of months because they are **proper nouns**.

Common Nouns	Proper Nouns
day, night, today, year, summer, spring, autumn, winter	**Days of the Week:** Monday, Tuesday, Wednesday, Thursday, Friday, Saturday, Sunday
	Months: January, February, March, April, May, June, July, August, September, October, November, December

Try It

A. Use proofreader's marks to correct the capitalization error in each sentence.

1. Last tuesday in English class, we read "A Job for Valentín."

2. The story is about a disabled man who gets a job at the pool for the Summer.

3. The pool in our community will open at the end of may.

4. Last Year, I took swimming lessons every Saturday.

5. By the beginning of Autumn, hardly anyone goes swimming.

B. (6–8) Pick one season and write at least three sentences describing activities you do during that season. Include days of the week and months.

_____

_____

_____

_____

Proofreader's Marks
Capitalize: school starts in August.
Do not capitalize: The Spring of 2005 was unusually hot.
See all Proofreader's Marks on page ix.

✓ Punctuate Appositives and Nouns of Direct Address Correctly

- An **appositive** is a noun or pronoun placed next to another noun to identify it or to give more information about it. An **appositive phrase** is an appositive plus any words that modify it. You should usually use commas to set off an appositive or an appositive phrase.

  Teresa, **the teenage narrator of the story**, learns not to judge others by their appearance.

  A playful young boy, Pablito makes friends wherever he goes.

- Use commas to set off a **noun of direct address**, or the person to whom one is speaking.

  Valentín, let me show you how to do that.

  Yes, **Teresa**, I am coming to help you.

Try It

A. For each sentence, add or delete a comma.

9. Valentín, the main character of the story looks after a little boy.

10. The boy's mother Maricela, thinks Valentín is not smart.

11. Teresa you will have a hard time teaching Valentín.

12. In the end, Valentín is the one, who teaches Teresa something new.

13. A caring person, Valentín helps save the young boy, from drowning.

B. Rewrite each sentence by including the appositive phrase. Use commas correctly.

14. Pablito does not know how to swim. **(appositive phrase: the young boy in the story)**

Pablito, the young boy in the story, does not know how to swim.

15. Valentín taught Teresa a valuable lesson. **(appositive phrase: a new employee)**

_____

Proofreader's Marks

Add comma:

"A Job for Valentín‸" a story by Judith Ortiz Cofer, is about a mentally challenged man.

Delete:

The story is about a man,⸝ who gets a job at the pool.

© National Geographic Learning, a part of Cengage Learning, Inc.

✔ Choose Active or Passive Voice

- A verb is in the active voice if the subject of the sentence does, or performs, the action. Most sentences are in the active voice.

    Judith Ortiz Cofer **writes** stories today.
    Saint Gildas **wrote** about Ambrosius in the 6th century.

- A verb is in the passive voice if the subject receives the action. A verb in the passive voice includes a form of the verb **be**, plus a form of the main verb.

    "A Job for Valentín" **was written** by Judith Ortiz Cofer.
    Arthur **was named** by a Welsh monk in the 9th century.

- Use **active voice** when you want to emphasize the subject. Use **passive voice** (1) when you want less emphasis on the subject, (2) when you don't know who the doer is, (3) when you don't want to mention the doer or place blame.

    Pablito **was pulled** from the pool by Valentín. (We know the doer.)
    Stories of Arthur **were told** before 500 C.E. (We don't know the doer.)
    Pablito **was left** alone near the pool. (We don't want to place blame.)

Try It

A. Read each sentence. Decide whether it should be written in the active voice or the passive voice. If it should be in the active voice, rewrite the sentence.

16. Valentín was chosen for the program. _____

_____

17. Permanent jobs at the pool were offered to us by Mrs. O'Brien. _____

_____

18. Mistakes about Valentín were made by Teresa. _____

_____

19. Valentín was born with a disability. _____

_____

Check for Consistency of Verb Tense

Check that you have used the correct verb tense and that you haven't switched from tense to tense. Change tense only if you talk about something that happened before or after the time you are writing about. The **present tense** of a verb tells about an action that is happening now. The **past tense** of a verb tells about an action that happened earlier or in the past.

Inconsistent verb tense: By the end of the story, she **realized** (past tense) that Valentín **teaches** (present tense) her to stop judging others by their appearance.

Consistent verb tense: By the end of the story, she **realized** (past tense) that Valentín **taught** (past tense) her to stop judging others by their appearance.

Try It

A. (20–25) Edit the story. Fix the six inconsistencies in verb tense.

I remember what I learn last summer when I volunteer at the animal shelter. I worked with a girl named Sabina. She hardly ever talked to me unless it was to tell me what to do. I think she was rude. Then one day, one of the cats, Boomer, ran out of the shelter. Sabina talked to me about how upset she was. I told her that together we would find Boomer. Sure enough, we find Boomer on the lawn, enjoying the sunny day. Sabina and I looked at each other and laughed. Now, we were good friends, and we remembered the good times we had last summer.

Proofreader's Marks

Delete:

Yesterday, I ~~get~~ got a new dog.

Add text:

   is
He ∧ very playful.

B. (26–30) Write at least five sentences about a lesson you learned. Did something happen that changed your opinion about someone? Be sure to use the correct verb tense.

_____

_____

_____

_____

_____

46 How Do I Show Possession?

One Way Is to Use a Possessive Noun.

- Use a **possessive noun** to show that someone owns, or possesses, something. Add **'s** if the possessive noun names one owner.

    Kathy reads the paper. **Kathy's** family reads *The City Daily*.

    Her **friend's** family reads *The Norwood Times*.

    Ted's teacher asks students to read articles aloud.

- A possessive noun can name more than one owner. Follow these rules:

    1. Add only an apostrophe if the plural noun ends in **-s**.

    The **students'** voices are expressive.

    2. Add **'s** if the plural noun does not end in **-s**.

    The **women's** magazine has a good health article.

Try It

A. Change the underlined words to a possessive noun. Write the possessive noun after each sentence.

1. The story about the politician was scandalous. _____

2. The coverage by the media was excellent. _____

3. The interest of readers was high. _____

4. Articles by writers told both sides of the story. _____

B. Rewrite each sentence to include a possessive noun.

5. The newspaper of my school is popular.

_____

6. Most articles by students teach me something new.

_____

7. Sometimes the articles change the views of people.

_____

C. Answer the questions about reading the newspaper. Use a possessive noun correctly in each sentence.

8. Do you often agree with your friend's opinions about the news? _____

_____

9. Are your family's opinions changed by what they read in newspapers? _____

_____

10. Do you gain people's respect because of what you learn from reading? _____

_____

D. (11–14) Write at least four more sentences about how reading newspapers helps you. Use possessive nouns in your response.

_____

_____

_____

_____

_____

Edit It

E. (15–20) Edit the letter. Fix six mistakes with **possessive nouns**.

Dear Tanya,

Last night, Terry's parents came to our house for dinner. Terrys' father was talking about a newspaper article at dinner. He disagreed with the authors views on poverty. My parents views were similar. After he expressed his opinion, I shared a few related facts from a newspaper article I had read. At first, I was scared to get involved in the adult's discussion. But I talked anyway. You should have seen my parent's faces'. They were really proud of me!

Your friend,

Rachel

Proofreader's Marks

Delete:

My family's views ~~are~~ similar.

Add an apostrophe:

The girls⌄ mom listened.

Transpose:

We read the man⧝U article.

See all Proofreader's Marks on page ix.

47 What's a Possessive Adjective?

It's an Ownership Word.

- Use a **possessive adjective** to tell who has or owns something. Put the possessive adjective before the **noun**.

    Tim is a graphic artist. He is **my** cousin.

    His job interests me. **Our** family includes many artists.

- Match the possessive adjective to the **noun** or **pronoun** that it goes with.

    Tim told me about **his** friends at the studio.
    noun

    They are all artists. **Their** artwork is impressive.
    pronoun

Subject Pronoun	Possessive Adjective
I	my
you	your
he	his
she	her
it	its
we	our
they	their

Try It

A. Complete each sentence about careers. Use the correct form.

1. _____ brother Arnold is a firefighter.
    Me / My

2. I visited _____ firehouse because I want to be a firefighter, too.
    he / his

3. Other firefighters also brought _____ families to work.
    they / their

4. One firefighter said, "_____ brother is very brave."
    You / Your

B. (5–8) Complete each sentence from the writer's point of view. Use possessive adjectives from the chart above.

I want to be a doctor, just like _____ mother. I know that

_____ city will need more doctors in the future. I asked my mother

about _____ education. I wondered if medical schools teach

_____ students different things today.

C. Answer these questions about careers. Use possessive adjectives.

9. Who do you talk to about his or her career? I talk with _____ about

_____.

10. What kind of job does that person have? _____

_____

11. How do their views change your opinion of their job? _____

_____

D. (12–15) Write at least four more sentences about people you know whose careers interest you. Use possessive adjectives in each sentence.

_____

_____

_____

_____

Edit It

E. (16–20) Edit the journal entry. Fix the five mistakes in possessive adjectives.

December 3

For my career report, I visited cousin Vito
at he job. Later I told me classmates all about
his job. We class has learned about many
careers, but Vito's job was awesome! He is an
oceanographer. When students heard that he
often works underwater, they jaws dropped.
They all had questions. Laura even said she
career plans changed after hearing my report.

Proofreader's Marks

Change text:

That is ^he career.
         his ℯ

See all Proofreader's Marks on page ix.

48 What Are the Possessive Pronouns?

Mine, Yours, His, Hers, Ours, and Theirs

Possessive Adjectives	my	your	his	her	our	their
Possessive Pronouns	mine	yours	his	hers	ours	theirs

Possessive adjectives are used before a noun.

Possessive pronouns stand alone.

My computer is fast.	This fast computer is **mine**.
That is **his** computer.	That computer is **his**.
There is **her** laptop.	That laptop is **hers**.
Our class meets on Thursdays.	The Thursday class is **ours**.
On Wednesdays, **their** class meets.	The Wednesday class is **theirs**.

Try It

A. Rewrite each sentence. Change the underlined words to the correct possessive pronoun.

1. I needed a computer, so my older sister let me use <u>her computer</u>. _____

_____

2. One day she said the computer was <u>my computer</u> to keep. _____

_____

3. Her company gave her one of <u>their computers</u>. _____

_____

4. I told my little brother that the computer was <u>our computer</u> to share. _____

_____

B. Complete each sentence with a possessive pronoun.

5. My neighbor works for a software company. That laptop computer is _____.

6. He taught me to use software. Now, I create computer games that are all _____.

7. My friends like my games better than _____.

8. I'd like to start a computer software business that is all _____.

9. My friend Julie wants to start a business that is all _____.

10. Maybe we can join together to create a software business that is all _____.

Write It

C. Answer the questions about computers and other technology. Use possessive pronouns.

11. Is the computer you work on yours or does it belong to your school? _____

_____

12. Do your friends depend more on their computers or their books to do homework? _____

_____

13. Do you have a calculator or other tools that you use to do your homework? _____

_____

14. Would you like to have a video camera that is all yours? Why? _____

_____

15. How could students use their computers to help them choose a college? _____

_____

D. (16–20) What special area of computer or other technology would you like to learn more about? Why? Write at least five sentences to explain. Use possessive pronouns.

_____

_____

_____

_____

_____

49 What's a Reflexive Pronoun?

It's a Word for the Same Person.

- Use a reflexive pronoun to talk about the same person or thing twice in a sentence. Reflexive pronouns end in -**self** or -**selves**.

  You know **yourself** and your study habits.

  Mary does not like to study by **herself**.

  Some students help **themselves** by studying in a group.

Reflexive Pronouns	
Singular	**Plural**
myself	ourselves
yourself	yourselves
himself,	themselves
herself, itself	

- Avoid these common mistakes with reflexive pronouns.

                      himself
  1. Hashid told ~~hisself~~ that he would ace the test.
                  themselves
  2. They get ~~theirselves~~ ready for the test.

Try It

A. Complete each sentence about joining a study group. Write the correct reflexive pronoun.

1. We must all prepare _____ for the big exam.
   ourselves / ourself

2. Karen and Kim prepare _____ by studying together.
   theirselves / themselves

3. Kim told me, "Help _____ by joining us."
   yourselves / yourself

B. Draw a line from each noun or pronoun to the correct reflexive pronoun.

4. We surprised   "You can be proud of yourselves."

5. The teacher said,   ourselves by getting top grades.

6. Kim said that now   she has more confidence in herself.

7. Other students were mad   at themselves for not joining our group.

Write It

C. Answer the questions about studying. Use reflexive pronouns.

8. What happens when you study by yourself? When I study by _____.

9. How do your friends study? They study by _____.

10. How is studying alone different from studying with others? _____

_____.

D. (11–14) Write at least four sentences that tell how a study group can help you and other students. Use reflexive pronouns correctly.

_____

_____

_____

_____

Edit It

E. (15–20) Edit the letter. Fix the six mistakes in reflexive pronouns.

Dear Parents,

Next week, students will take a final math exam. They must prepare themselves for the test. Students can study by theirselves, but study groups can help. You are welcome to set up study groups by ourselves. I will also make me available for private tutoring. Last year, one student gave himselves an extra boost by joining two study groups. Many students later adopted the same strategy for theirself. We can count ourselfs lucky that our students are so hardworking.

Sincerely,

Ms. Juarez

Proofreader's Marks

Change text:

myself
I will study by ~~yourself.~~

See all Proofreader's Marks on page ix.

⑤⓪ Show Possession

Remember: Use possessive words to show that someone owns something. A possessive adjective comes before a noun. A possessive pronoun stands alone.

Possessive Adjectives	my	your	his	her	its	our	your	their
Possessive Pronouns	mine	yours	his	hers		ours	yours	theirs

Try It

A. Complete each sentence. Write the correct possessive word.

1. My sister has seizures sometimes. This problem is not only _____.
   her/hers

2. Our family needs to be prepared. _____ reading helps me to
   Mine/My
   understand the disease.

3. _____ warning signs are easy to miss. We must learn as much as
   Their/Its
   possible.

4. What I learn does not just have an effect on _____ health. It makes
   her/hers
   me much more aware of health issues.

5. My reading inspires me. I now understand that the responsibility for my own health is
   _____.
   my/mine

6. _____ whole family is closer now. That is because we all work
   Our/Ours
   together to help my sister.

7. My sister is more confident. She feels the disease is not just _____.
   her/hers

111

B. **(8–12) Read the interview between two students for the school paper. Complete sentences with mine, hers, ours, yours, or theirs.**

Q. Whom have you helped with _____ research?

A. My friend Jackie asked me to do research about diabetes on my computer. _____ was broken. Diabetes was her problem, not _____, but I was happy to help.

Q. How did what you learn help Jackie?

A. I told Jackie about a girl with diabetes who posted her story online. Jackie said the girl had experiences similar to _____, which made her feel less alone. I also learned that exercise can help. My sister and I decided to walk with Jackie every day after school. Those walks not only made her body stronger, they strengthened _____, too.

Write It

C. **Answer the questions about your health knowledge. Use possessive adjectives and pronouns.**

13. What do you learn from friends or family with medical conditions? Explain. _____

_____

14. Have you helped friends or family to learn more about their conditions? How? _____

_____

15. What health issue concerns your family the most? _____

_____

16. Do you think people in general do enough research about their own health? _____

_____

D. **(17–20) Write at least four sentences about something you have learned recently that you use to stay healthy. Use possessive adjectives and pronouns.**

_____

_____

_____

_____

_____

51 What Kinds of Things Do Prepositions Show?

Location, Direction, and Time

Prepositions That Show Location: in, on top of, on, at, over, under, above, below, next to, beside, in front of, in back of, behind

- Use a preposition of **location** to tell where something is.

   Hector's mom keeps her old books **under** her bed.
   She keeps them **in** a big box.

Prepositions That Show Direction: into, throughout, up, down, through, across, to

- Use a preposition of **direction** to tell where something is going.

   Hector's sister Sonrisa reaches **into** the box and takes out a book.
   She and Hector look **through** the box to find something good to read.

Prepositions That Show Time: after, until, before, during

- Use a preposition of **time** to tell when something happens.

   Sonrisa finds a book **before** dinner. Hector finds his book **after** dinner.

Try It

A. Complete each sentence about reading a book. Add a preposition.

1. Hector starts to read the book _____ the bus.

2. He sees that his mother has written her name _____ the book.

3. Donna is sitting _____ Hector.

4. He holds the book _____ her so she can see it, too.

B. Complete each sentence about reading a book. Choose the correct preposition.

5. The book is about a teenager in California _____ the 1960s.
   during/on

6. Donna tells Hector that she wants to go _____ California.
   at/to

7. Hector says he wants to live _____ the ocean someday.
   beside/in

C. Answer the questions about reading. Use prepositions.

8. At what time of day do you usually read? _____

9. Where do you read? _____

10. What do you do with books after you read them? _____

11. Where do you get most of your books? _____

12. Do your friends or family recommend books to you after they have read them?_____

_____

D. (13–17) Write at least five sentences that tell about the books you most enjoy reading. Use prepositions.

_____

_____

_____

_____

_____

Edit It

E. (18–25) Edit the letter. Fix the eight mistakes in prepositions.

Dear Uncle Bernie,

    Thank you for the great book. I loved reading something you read during your teenage years. I also like science fiction stories about life in other planets. I gave the book over my friend Tim until school. He took it at his house. Don't worry, he will return it during next Friday. I can't wait before your next visit! Will that be above Saturday? I can return the book under your visit.

Your nephew,

Aaron

Proofreader's Marks

Change text:
I read ~~before~~ after dinner.
         ^

See all Proofreader's Marks on page ix.

52 How Do You Recognize a Prepositional Phrase?

Look for the Preposition.

- A **phrase** is a group of related words. A **prepositional phrase** begins with a preposition and ends with a noun or pronoun. Use prepositional phrases to add information to your sentences.

  Victor walked **through the library**.
                                    noun

  He waved **to Felix** who sat **near the window**.
                noun   **noun**

- The **noun** at the end of a prepositional phrase is called the **object of the preposition**.

Try It

A. Add a prepositional phrase to tell more.

1. Victor found the book. He found the book _____.

2. He read the story. He read the story _____.

3. Alex liked the book's setting. He liked the book's setting _____.

4. His sister liked the picture. She liked the picture _____.

5. Alex showed the book. He showed the book _____.

B. (6–11) Write a prepositional phrase to complete each sentence. You may use the same preposition more than once.

Victor finds an exciting new novel _____. The story takes place _____. He shows it to Paco. Paco looks quickly _____. He hands it back _____. He says that his family is going _____. He wants to read a book about Spain. Victor puts the book back _____.

C. Answer the questions below about your school library. Use prepositional phrases.

12. Where is the library in your school? _____

13. Are there many books on the shelves? _____

14. Where do you like to sit in the library? _____

15. Do you sit near your friends? _____

16. When do you go to the library? _____

D. (17–20) Write at least four sentences that describe what your school library looks like. Use prepositional phrases.

_____

_____

_____

_____

_____

Edit It

E. (21–25) Edit the letter. Fix the five mistakes in prepositional phrases.

Dear Lillie,

    Yesterday, I found some old postcards in the garage. The message under the back of one of the cards reads "Dear Mother, last night we pitched our tents over the Mariposa Grove of Big Trees in Yosemite Valley. One tree is 90 feet around!" Lillie, this card is so exciting! It makes me want to go at Yosemite Valley soon. Yosemite Valley is located over California. It will be fun to camp for that tree.

Love,

Pat

Proofreader's Marks
Change text:
inside
We stood ~~over~~ the tree.
See all Proofreader's Marks on page ix.

53 Can I Use a Pronoun After a Preposition?

Yes, Use an Object Pronoun.

- Use an **object pronoun** after a preposition.

    This is a good job **for me**.

    Dad discusses the interview **with me**.

Object Pronouns	
Singular	Plural
me	us
you	you
him, her, it	them

Try It

A. (1–5) Read this paragraph about preparing for a job interview. Add object pronouns.

Dad brought home a book about careers for _____. He showed me the part about gardening. He thought it would help me with my job interview. I read carefully through _____. Then Dad had me discuss the information with _____. The interview was in the morning. I felt well prepared for _____. Dad wished me luck. He said, "I'll be rooting for _____!"

B. Complete each sentence. Choose the correct object pronoun.

6. The interviewer had many questions for _____.
   me / you

7. I thought I had good answers for _____.
   it / him

8. He said, "I think you will fit right in with _____."
   him / us

9. He added, "This is the perfect job for _____."
   her / you

10. He said, "Welcome aboard" and smiled at _____.
    me / you

C. Answer the questions about how reading can be helpful. Use object pronouns.

11. What helpful advice can you find in books? _____

12. Have you recommended useful books to a friend? _____

D. (13–15) Write at least three sentences that tell more about how reading books can help you. Use object pronouns.

_____

_____

_____

_____

Edit It

E. (16–20) Edit the journal entry. Fix the five mistakes with object pronouns.

March 14

It was a good day for me. It wasn't such a
good day for Tarik and Elicia. Everything
seemed to go totally wrong for her. Our
teacher, Mrs. Sweeney, gave them good
advice about their upcoming job interviews.
Unfortunately, Elicia did not listen to them.
She didn't get the job. Tarik read the book he
got from you, but he started off late for the
interview. The interviewer looked at his watch.
Him saw that Tarik was ten minutes late. Tarik
wants to sell clothes in that store. I hope he
made that clear to me!

Proofreader's Marks

Change text:

My interview is ~~in~~ Tuesday.
            on

See all Proofreader's Marks on page ix.

54 In a Prepositional Phrase, Where Does the Pronoun Go?

It Goes Last.

- A **prepositional phrase** starts with a preposition and ends with a noun or pronoun. Sometimes, it ends with both. Put the pronoun last.

  Cousin Marilyn showed a book **to my mom and me**.

  It was about living **in Sydney, Australia**. She loaned the book to my dad. She gave it **to him** last night.

- You can put a prepositional phrase at the start of the sentence to emphasize your idea.

  For her, moving to Australia is an important goal.

- Avoid these common mistakes in a prepositional phrase:

  1. Use **me**, not **I**:

  Not having Marilyn around would be sad for my parents and ~~I~~.
        me

  2. Put **me** last:

  my parents and me

  She is important to ~~me and my parents~~.

Try It

A. Complete each sentence. Use the correct pronouns.

1. Marilyn said the move was an adventure for her family and _____.
she / her

2. She added that she would always write to _____.
us and her friends / her friends and us

3. For my parents and _____, thinking about Australia was exciting.
me / I

4. My mom explained, "You are important to my husband and _____."
me / I

5. However, they were very excited for _____.
she / her

6. For _____, Marilyn's move to Australia is sad.
we / us

B. Complete each sentence. Use the correct pronouns.

7. Marilyn said we could visit her family and _____.

8. For my parents and _____, that was a wonderful invitation.

9. She thought our visit would be good for her and _____.

10. My father said, "That invitation means a lot to my wife and _____."

11. I said, "For Marilyn and _____, this visit will be very special."

Write It

C. Answer the questions about going places. Use pronouns correctly.

12. What place have you read about that you would like to see with your family? I have read about _____.

13. What would be fun for all of you to do in that place? _____
    _____

14. Would moving to that place be a big change for you and your family? _____
    _____

15. What effect might the move have on your friends and you? _____
    _____

D. (16–20) Write at least five sentences that tell more about a place you would like to visit or live in with your family. Use pronouns correctly.

_____

_____

_____

_____

_____

_____

55 Use Pronouns in Prepositional Phrases

Remember: You can use prepositions to add details to your sentences. If you need a pronoun in a prepositional phrase, use an object pronoun.

Sentences with Prepositional Phrases

- I have books **about science, countries, and famous people**.

- Books have special importance **to me**.

- Many of the books are **for my sister and me**.

- My grandparents gave most of the books **to us** as presents.

Object Pronouns	
Singular	**Plural**
me	us
you	you
him, her, it	them

Try It

A. Add a noun or an object pronoun to complete each prepositional phrase.

1. I have one book about _____.

2. My grandfather is a biologist, and he gave the book to _____.

3. The book about dancers is for _____ and _____.

4. My grandparents gave it to _____ when we were little.

5. We used to create silly dance performances for _____.

6. That book brings back fond memories for _____ all.

B. Complete each sentence. Use the correct pronouns.

7. My grandparents always give nice gifts to _____ and _____.

8. For _____, the books were the most special gifts.

9. When I was little, my grandmother made a cookbook for both of _____.

10. We used it to bake a birthday cake for _____.

C. Answer the questions about books. Use prepositional phrases with object pronouns.

11. For you, are books very important? _____

12. What kinds of books are special for you? _____

13. Did people give some of those books to you? Who? _____

14. Do the books bring back good memories for you? Explain. _____

15. What other kinds of books might be interesting for you to collect? _____

D. (16–20) Write at least five sentences that describe more about books that are important to you. Use prepositional phrases with object pronouns.

_____

_____

_____

_____

_____

_____

Edit It

E. (21–25) Edit the paragraph. Fix five mistakes in prepositional phrases.

My friend Emanuel says that books are important to him. I agree! To we, the library is an exciting place. The range of subjects in the library is interesting for me and Emanuel. I like the books on nature and animals. For I, these books are the best. Emanuel prefers books on space exploration. To he, space is exciting. I said, "Emanuel, here is a book about taking animals on a space flight. This book would be great for you and I. Let's check it out!"

Proofreader's Marks

Change text:

Books are interesting to you and I. me
        ^

See all Proofreader's Marks on page ix.

56 When Do You Use an Indefinite Pronoun?

When You Can't Be Specific

- When you are not talking about a specific person or thing, you can use an **indefinite pronoun**.

   Someone can teach you to read. **Anyone** here can help you.

- Some indefinite pronouns are always singular, so they need a **singular verb** that ends in **-s**.

   Everything seems to be ready. **Everybody wants** to learn.

Singular Indefinite Pronouns

another	each	everything	nothing
anybody	either	neither	somebody
anyone	everybody	nobody	someone
anything	everyone	no one	something

Try It

A. Complete each sentence about reading. Use the correct form of the verb.

1. My friends and I read about someone who _____ to read.

want/wants

2. No one _____ that Ken cannot read.

know/knows

3. Everything _____ difficult for him.

is/are

4. Ken hopes something _____ soon.

change/changes

B. (5–9) Complete each sentence. Use indefinite pronouns from the chart above.

My friends and I want to help _____ like Ken. We volunteer at the literacy center and do _____ to help. _____ in our families can read. _____ who cannot read has fears. _____ is more important than helping people read.

Write It

C. Answer the questions about literacy. Use indefinite pronouns correctly in each sentence.

10. Have you ever helped anyone learn to read? _____

11. How do you think someone who can't read might feel about literacy centers? _____

_____

D. (12–15) Write at least four sentences about how learning to read can help someone. Use indefinite pronouns in your response.

_____

_____

_____

_____

_____

Edit It

E. (16–20) Edit the journal entry. Fix five mistakes in indefinite pronouns.

October 17

Almost everyone I know volunteers at the literacy center. They all want to help nobody who cannot read. At the center, everybody has to feel ashamed. The atmosphere is supportive. Nobody can go to the center. Once they learn to read, anything gets easier. They realize how much fun reading can be. Then anyone feels better. I'm glad that I'm able to help change people's lives.

Proofreader's Marks

Change text:

Everyone
~~Nobody~~ can learn to read.

See all Proofreader's Marks on page ix.

57 Which Indefinite Pronouns Are Plural?

Both, Few, Many, and Several

- Use an **indefinite pronoun** when you are not talking about a specific person or thing.

  Several of the scientists in our city check our water supply.

  Many of the people in our town have been sick lately.

Plural Indefinite Pronouns	
both	many
few	several

- Some **indefinite pronouns** are always plural, so they need a **plural verb**.

  A **few** of our top scientists **talk** to the two government officials about the problem.

  Both of the officials **insist** that the situation is not serious.

Try It

A. Complete each sentence about water pollution. Use the correct form of the verb.

1. Many of the scientists who study the ocean _____ that our water supplies are polluted.
   warn / warns

2. A few _____ the water in our local reservoir.
   study / studies

3. Both of the lakes in our city _____ also polluted.
   is / are

4. Several of our rivers _____ evidence of contamination.
   show / shows

5. Many of the people I know _____ eating fish from our lakes altogether.
   avoid / avoids

6. A few still _____ fish from the rivers occasionally.
   eat / eats

B. Complete each sentence with a verb from the box.

agree	are	need	tell	volunteer

7. A few of the people in my city _____ really knowledgeable about water pollution.

8. They feel that both of our top scientists _____ to be part of the solution.

9. Both of my brothers _____ that clean water is important.

10. Many of my friends _____ on weekends to clean up the lake.

11. Several of them _____ me I am welcome to join them.

Write It

C. Answer these questions about water pollution. Use the correct form of the verb.

12. Are several of your friends concerned about water pollution? _____

13. Do you think many of the students in your school know about the problem? _____

    _____

14. What are a few of the steps people can take to stop water pollution? _____

    _____

15. Do you think that adults and young people should help solve the problem? How can both of them work together? _____

    _____

D. (16–20) Write at least five sentences about your views on water pollution. Use indefinite pronouns and verbs correctly in each sentence.

_____

_____

_____

_____

_____

126

58 Which Indefinite Pronouns Are Tricky?

The Ones That Can Be Singular or Plural

- The **indefinite pronouns** in the chart can be either singular or plural.

- The **prepositional phrase** after the pronoun shows whether the sentence talks about one thing or more than one thing. Use the correct **verb**.

Singular or Plural Indefinite Pronouns	
all	none
any	some
most	

Singular:	**Most** of the work **is** ahead of us.
Plural:	**Most** of the scientists **are** concerned.
Singular:	**Some** of the research **is** in progress.
Plural:	**Most** of the students **are** involved.
Singular:	**All** of the country **is** at risk.
Plural:	**All** of the experts **are** in agreement.

Try It

A. Complete each sentence about pollution. Use the correct form of the verb.

1. Some of the studies _____ the causes of air pollution.
     reveal / reveals

2. Most of the scientists _____ that cars are part of the problem.
     agree / agrees

3. Any of the solutions _____ worth exploring.
     is / are

4. None of the work _____ wasted.
     is / are

5. Some of my neighbors _____ to do their part.
     try / tries

6. A few people _____ to work instead of drive.
     walk / walks

B. Complete each sentence about car pollution with the correct form of a verb.

7. Most of our local pollution _____ from cars.

8. All of the cars _____ to be more efficient.

9. Most of my neighbors _____ cleaner air.

10. Some of my friends _____ mass transit.

Write It

C. Answer the questions about pollution. Use indefinite pronouns and verbs correctly.

11. Are most of your neighbors concerned about air pollution? _____

_____

12. Do some of your friends drive cars? _____

_____

13. Do all of the cars pollute the air? Explain? _____

_____

14. Are any of the scientists in your city working to find solutions for the problem? _____

_____

15. Do all of the scientists agree about the causes of pollution? _____

_____

D. (16–20) What special area of air, water, or other pollution would you like to learn more about? Why? Write at least five sentences to explain. Use indefinite pronouns and verbs correctly.

_____

_____

_____

_____

_____

_____

59 What's an "Antecedent"?

It's the Word a Pronoun Refers To.

- A **pronoun** usually refers back to a noun. This noun is called the **antecedent**.

  Mr. Howard teaches me to play guitar. **He** is a good teacher.
  antecedent   pronoun

- A pronoun must **agree** with its antecedent. This means that the pronoun has to go with the noun it refers to.

  My **guitar** is new. **It** sounds beautiful.

  My **family** loves to hear me practice. **They** enjoy music.

Try It

A. Identify the antecedent for the underlined pronoun. Add a sentence using the pronoun.

1. Mr. Harrison tells me to practice. He says that practice helps me learn. _____

   _____

2. My brother and I play music together. We both love to play. _____

   _____

3. Music is my favorite activity. It is important to me. _____

   _____

4. My cousins also play music. They play piano and violin. _____

   _____

B. Add a sentence to each item to continue the idea of the first sentence. Use the correct pronoun for each underlined antecedent.

5. My mother likes Mr. Harrison. _____

6. My teacher has many students. _____

7. My brother and I want to teach music someday, too. _____

C. Answer the questions about learning a skill. Include pronouns and the correct antecedents.

8. What skill would you like to learn? I would like to _____.

9. Who would you like to study with? _____

10. Would you like to use this skill in your career? Explain. _____

D. (11–14) Write at least four sentences about someone who is skilled in your area of interest. Use pronouns and antecedents correctly.

_____

_____

_____

_____

_____

Edit It

E. (15–20) Edit the journal entry. Fix the six mistakes in pronouns.

November 14

Aunt Roberta let me paint with her today. We is a really fine artist. My aunt shows her paintings in a gallery. He is a big space in a fancy building. Many people buy her paintings. She love the way she paints landscapes. Her paintings are large. It are sometimes more than four feet wide! Painting is the career I want to have. They is not always easy, but it is what I love. Aunt Roberta and my cousin Arnie are both artists. He both said they will teach me to paint.

Proofreader's Marks

Change text:

Arnie paints. ~~They~~ He is an artist.

See all Proofreader's Marks on page ix.

60 Use the Correct Pronoun

Remember: When you use a pronoun, be sure it fits correctly into the sentence. Also be sure it goes with the noun it refers to.

- Use a **subject pronoun** in the subject of a sentence. Use an **object pronoun** after the verb or after a preposition.

    Larry talks to **Karen**. **He** tells **her** how he reached his career goal.

    His **friends** chose the same **career**. **They** love **it**.

- All **pronouns** must agree with the **noun** they refer to. This noun is called the antecedent.
    1. If the noun names a male, use **he** or **him**.
    2. If the noun names a female, use **she** or **her**.
    3. If a noun names one thing, use **it** or **it**.
    4. If a noun names "more than one," use **they** or **them**.

Try It

A. Complete each sentence. Write the correct pronouns.

1. Larry has a good job. _____ worked hard to get it.

He / They

2. Larry told his sister how he reached his goal. He spent years preparing for

   _____.

it / them

3. Students in high school must take science. They must be good at

   _____.

it / them

4. Teens should study biology. They need a strong background in _____.

it / them

5. Hospitals are happy to have young volunteers. They can offer good medical experience to

   _____.

it / them

B. (6–9) Complete each sentence. Use the correct subject and object pronouns.

Larry worked for Dr. Lehrer in high school. _____ learned a lot from

_____. After his junior year, Larry attended a special summer program.

_____ was a medical school program for teens. The program helped

_____ see if they might want to become doctors.

Write It

C. Answer the questions about career goals. Use subject and object pronouns correctly.

10. Who do you know who has reached an important career goal? _____

11. What types of things did that person have to learn in order to reach that goal? _____

_____

12. What steps did they take to prepare for their career? _____

_____

D. (13–16) Write at least four sentences about a career that interests you. Discuss at least two things you would have to learn to reach that goal. Use subject and object pronouns correctly.

_____

_____

_____

Edit It

E. (17–20) Edit the letter. Fix the five mistakes with pronouns.

Dear Dr. Larry Harris,

I am delighted to offer you a position. Your job begins on
September 3rd. They will involve three main responsibilities. It are
examination, diagnosis, and treatment. Mr. Harris is the head of
your department. Him will be happy to answer questions. You will
receive pension benefits. Them begin on your first day.

Sincerely,

Dr. Julian Ottavio

Proofreader's Marks
Change text:
He
~~Him~~ is a doctor.
See all Proofreader's Marks on page ix.

132   © National Geographic Learning, a part of Cengage Learning, Inc.

Edit and
Proofread

✓ Capitalize the Titles of Publications

- Capitalize all main words in the titles of publications, such as books, magazines, newspapers, and articles.
  Book: *Successful Television Writing*
  Magazine: *Electronic House*
  Newspaper: *USA Today*
  Article: "Bonus Features Aid TV DVD Craze"
- Do not capitalize **a**, **on**, **the**, or **of** unless it is the first word in the title.
  Television: Technology and Cultural Form
  The New York Times

Try It

A. Use proofreader's marks to correct the capitalization error in each sentence.

1. My uncle reads *The Wall street Journal*.

2. I am halfway through *Fifty Years Of Television*.

3. I e-mailed you an article. It's called "Will Reality TV survive?"

B. Answer each question. Be sure to capitalize titles correctly.

4. What is the name of your school newspaper?

   _____

5. What textbook do you use in your science class?

   _____

6. What is the name of your favorite magazine?

   _____

Proofreader's Marks

Capitalize:

He reads the *Chicago sun-times.*

Do not capitalize:

My favorite book is *Gone With The Wind.*

See all Proofreader's Marks on page ix.

✓ Use Parentheses Correctly

- Use **parentheses** to set off a sentence or phrase that interrupts an idea. This includes citations in research reports.

   Americans (according to ACNielsen) watch more than four hours of TV each day. That means they watch twenty-eight hours per week (Herr 8).

- Place end punctuation after the end parenthesis of a citation or interrupting phrase.

   American children spend 1,500 hours per year watching TV (compared with 900 hours per year attending school).

   They also see approximately 30,000 TV commercials per year (Hartung 23).

- Place the end quotation mark for a direct quotation before the citation in parentheses.

   In years to come, "Americans will spend half their lives watching TV, going online, listening to music, and reading" (Kornblum A5).

Try It

A. (7–10) Fix the four errors in punctuation. Use proofreader's marks.

   Most people think it began with *Survivor*, but reality TV has actually been around for nearly as long as television itself late 1930s . The phenomenon began in 1948 with a show called *Candid Camera* Jacobs 52 . Created and hosted by Allen Funt, the show featured ordinary Americans who found themselves in perplexing situations, which were set up by the show's producers. These scenarios usually involved trick props a desk with drawers that randomly pop open, for example or some other type of prank. In one episode, Funt "pretended to be an airport security person and instructed passengers to go down the conveyor belt through a fake X-ray machine (Jacobs 146)". The show's victims would be confused and sometimes angry until they heard the famous tag line: "Smile! You're on Candid Camera!"

Proofreader's Marks
Add parentheses: The first television was built in 1927 (Jones 15).
Add quotation marks: "I saw you on TV last night," she said.
Delete: I like ~~like~~ reality TV.

✔ Use Consistent Verb Tense

- Do not change tenses in a paragraph or essay unless you are talking about something that happened before or after the time that you are writing about.

    Right now, I **want** to watch my favorite TV show. I **taped** it last night because I was busy studying for a test.

- In general, use the **past tense** to tell a story about historical events.

    The first television broadcast **appeared** in London in 1938.

    Once upon a time, there **lived** a family who **didn't own** a television set. They **had** conversations with each other and **read** books to entertain themselves.

- Use the **present tense** to talk about statistics; literary, film, and television works; actions that happen on a regular basis; and your own ideas.

    Ninety-nine percent of households in the United States **have** at least one television set.

    Jayden **watches** one hour of television every night.

    I **believe** that Americans **need** to watch less television.

Try It

A. (11–15) Fix the five inconsistencies in verb tense. Use proofreader's marks.

In the early 1950s, the most popular form of television comedy was the comedy-variety show, which transfers easily to television from radio. This type of show is usually hosted by a celebrity. One of the most famous early comedy-variety shows was *The Texaco Star Theater* with Milton Berle as host.

In the late 1950s, however, a new form of television comedy became popular—the situation comedy, or sitcom. This form really took off with the production of *I Love Lucy*, starring Lucille Ball and Desi Arnaz. The show revolutionized the television industry: It is the first program filmed in California instead of New York; it is the first program filmed with the three-camera technique; and, it sets the basic plotline for situation comedies for years to come.

Proofreader's Marks
Change text:
What ~~were~~ *are* you watching?

✓ Make Pronouns Agree with Their Antecedents

- A **pronoun** usually refers back to a noun. This noun is called the **antecedent**.

  Where is the **remote**? Isn't **it** on the coffee table?

  antecedent   pronoun

- A pronoun must **agree** with its antecedent. It must match the noun it refers to in gender (male or female) and number (singular or plural).

  Jorge still can't find the remote. **He** has looked everywhere.

  Ask **Rachel and Vanessa**. **They** were watching TV this afternoon.

Try It

A. **(16–21) Complete the story by adding the correct pronouns. Draw an arrow from each pronoun to its antecedent.**

Eugene McDonald was the founder of Zenith Electronics Corporation. _____

wanted to give people a way to control their TVs from their couches. _____

met with Zenith's engineers and asked _____ to come up with an idea.

_____ created a device called the Lazy Bones. _____ was

connected to the TV by a cable. _____ was very awkward to use.

B. **(22–25) Edit the report. Fix the four pronouns. Use proofreader's marks.**

McDonald wanted something better. It went back to the engineers
and told him to create a remote without wires. One engineer,
Eugene Polley, created a remote that used a light beam to control
the TV. She became known as the Flashmatic. Unfortunately, the
TV didn't just respond to the Flashmatic. They also responded to
sunlight, which caused the TV to turn on and off by itself.

Proofreader's Marks

Change text:
it's
Can you fix him?

61 What Are Adjectives?

They Are Describing Words.

- You can describe people, places, or things with **adjectives** . They answer the question: What is it like?

- Use adjectives to describe

    1. how something looks: **strange, bumpy, threatening, gigantic**

    2. how something sounds: **loud, shrill, metallic**

    3. how something feels, tastes, or smells: **rough, fresh, salty**

    4. a person's mood: **tired, optimistic, sad, angry**

- Adjectives help the reader visualize what you are writing about. The **ominous** clouds blew across the already **darkening** sky. **Roaring** thunder was preceded by **sharp** daggers of lightning.

Try It

A. Add excitement to the story about the unexpected storm. Use adjectives from the box.

| explosive | frightened | horrendous | howling | sudden |

1. The _____ storm was unexpected.

2. I heard an _____ noise, and the lights went out.

3. The _____ silence disturbed me.

4. Then the _____ wind began to screech outside my windows.

5. My _____ dogs hid under the bed.

B. Now think of your own adjectives. Write them to complete the sentences.

6. Usually, I don't mind storms, but this _____ storm was scaring me.

7. I heard every _____ sound and jumped.

8. Was an _____ stranger in the house with me?

137

C. Answer the questions to tell about a time when something unexpected happened when you were home alone. Use at least one adjective in each answer.

9. What happened? I _____

_____.

10. Were you scared? Why? _____

_____

11. How did you handle the situation? _____

_____

D. (12–15) Write at least four sentences to tell about a time the power went out unexpectedly during a storm. Use adjectives in your sentences.

_____

_____

_____

_____

_____

E. (16–20) Improve the journal entry. Add five adjectives.

September 30

Tonight, a scary thing happened to me. I was home all alone when we had a storm. My house lost power. I heard noises all evening long. The only light I had was the light from my flashlight. My dogs just hid under the bed. I sat alone in the house until my parents came home.

Proofreader's Marks

Add text: howling
There was a wind.

See all Proofreader's Marks on page ix.

62 Where Do Adjectives Appear in a Sentence?

Usually Before the Noun

- Often the **adjective** comes before the **noun** you are describing.
  The **dark house** made **creaky noises**.
  The **pounding rain** broke the **eerie silence**.

- If two adjectives both describe the noun, separate them with a comma (,).
  Cold, clammy air filled the house.
  I sat and hoped that the **furious, windy rain** would soon end.

Try It

A. Write adjectives to complete the sentences.

1. Besides scaring me, this storm was causing another _____ problem.

2. I had a _____, _____ history paper due the next day.

3. I was sitting in my _____ house in _____ darkness, though.

4. My normally _____ computer was quiet.

5. I worried about the _____, _____ zero I was going to get on my paper.

B. (6–12) Write adjectives to complete the paragraph.

Finally, at around 10 o'clock, the _____ wind died down. The _____, _____ rain stopped. A short while later, my _____ dogs ventured out from under the bed! But best of all, the lights came on. I spent a very _____ night completing my _____ homework, and I learned not to put things off until the _____ moment.

C. Complete each sentence to describe a storm. Use adjectives.

13. One _____ day, _____.

14. The _____, _____ sky _____.

15. My _____, _____ family and I _____

    _____.

16. The storm was like a _____.

D. (17–20) Write at least four sentences about a time when you put off homework and then something unexpected happened. Use adjectives in each sentence.

_____

_____

_____

_____

_____

Edit It

E. (21–25) Improve the news article. Add five adjectives.

Devastating Storm Blacks Out Region

The whole region suffered the effects of last night's storm. Houses and businesses all over the state lost power. The winds caused trees to topple and power lines to fall. Today, some people have their power back. Many other people are still sitting in the dark.

Proofreader's Marks

Add text:

unfortunate
Many people are still
without power.

See all Proofreader's Marks on page ix.

63 How Do You Use a Predicate Adjective?

After a Form of the Verb *Be*

- Most of the time, **adjectives** come before **nouns**.

  A **scary event** happened to me yesterday.

- If the verb is a form of **be**, you can put the adjective after the verb. The forms of **be** are **am**, **is**, **are**, **was**, and **were**.

  The **event** was **scary**. At first, **I** was **worried**.

- If you use two predicate adjectives, join them with **and**, **but**, or **or**.

  Yesterday, I was **shocked and nervous**. Today, I am **anxious but excited**.
  Are you **jittery or relaxed** when you perform?

Try It

A. Use adjectives from the box to complete the sentences.

| fantastic | horrified | ready | sick | surprised | thrilled |

1. Yesterday, I was _____ to get a call from the play's director.

2. She told me that the lead actor was _____.

3. She asked me, "Are you _____ to stand in for him?"

4. I was _____ but _____.

5. This opportunity was _____ for me.

B. Now think of your own adjectives. Write them to complete the sentences.

6. I am _____ and _____ on opening night.

7. I am not _____, though.

8. I am _____ and _____ with my lines.

9. It is _____ to get up on stage.

10. On the other hand, the experience is _____ and _____.

Write It

C. Complete each sentence to tell about a time when you had to suddenly prepare for an unexpected event. Use predicate adjectives.

11. I was _____ and _____ when _____
_____.

12. The experience was _____ because _____
_____.

13. Now I am _____ that it happened because _____
_____.

D. (14–16) Write at least three sentences about something unexpected that could happen during a school performance or sports event. Use predicate adjectives.

_____

_____

_____

_____

_____

Edit It

E. (17–20) Edit the play review for the school newspaper. Add four predicate adjectives.

Last night's play was both scary and terrific. The actors were. The lead actor had only three days to learn the role. This reviewer thinks he did an incredible job. His acting was. My recommendation is that you see this play before closing night. I am that I did. You will find that the play is very.

Proofreader's Marks

Add text:
                happy
I was to be in the play.

See all Proofreader's Marks on page ix.

64 Why Do You Use a Demonstrative Adjective?

To Point Something Out

- A **demonstrative adjective** signals where something is—either near or far.
- Use **this** and **these** for something near you.
  This play has fantastic props.
  I helped make **these props** here.
- Use **that** and **those** for something far from you.
  Did you like **that prop** over there at the back of the stage?
  I think **those props** over there are scary.

Demonstrative Adjectives	
Singular	Plural
this	these
that	those

Try It

A. Write the correct demonstrative adjective to complete each sentence.

1. The audience really enjoyed _____ play.
   this / these

2. _____ actor on the other side of the room was so scary.
   This / That

3. I jumped out of my seat when _____ loud noises blared.
   that / those

4. I wasn't expecting _____ bright light display, either.
   that / those

5. Both of _____ things helped build up the suspense.
   that / those

6. The surprise caused by _____ special effects was incredible.
   this / these

7. Everyone in _____ audience screamed.
   this / that

8. I think _____ special effects in this play are the best ever!
   these / those

B. Fix the demonstrative adjective in each sentence.

9. The main character in these play turns into a monster.

10. In this three acts right here, he is a man.

11. Then he puts on these scary costume over there.

12. These sharp fangs that you see over there startled me.

13. This special effects here built up suspense, too.

14. All of these costumes and special effects that we saw earlier made the play more frightening.

Write It

C. Answer the questions about your favorite special effects from a movie you have seen. Use demonstrative adjectives.

15. Were the special effects scary? _____

   _____

16. How would you describe the special effects? _____

   _____

17. Why did you like them? _____

   _____

D. (18–20) Write at least three sentences about a scary scene in a movie you have seen. Use demonstrative adjectives.

   _____

   _____

   _____

   _____

   _____

65 Use Adjectives to Elaborate

Remember: Use adjectives to add interesting, lively details to your writing. Adjectives help readers see, hear, touch, smell, and taste.

See	Hear	Touch	Smell	Taste
enormous	metallic	icy	burnt	salty
red	shrill	rough	smoky	sour
shiny	whistling	sticky	sweet	spicy

secondhand   deserted   spooky

Oh, no! My car just died on the ~~unused~~ highway near the ~~dark~~ woods.

Try It

A. Write adjectives to make the sentences more interesting.

1. My friends and I were _____ and _____ as we waited for help to arrive.

2. We sat in the _____ darkness with only the _____ moon for light.

3. One friend was telling us about the _____ bear that had wandered into her yard.

4. All of a sudden, I heard _____ noises coming from the woods.

5. Were those _____, _____ noises a bear?

B. (6–12) Write adjectives to make the paragraph more interesting.

My friend kept on telling her story. Now I was really _____! What would we do if a _____, _____ bear came out of the woods? My _____ imagination went to work. I thought of all the _____ animals stalking us, and I headed back to the _____ car. I felt safer there. I was really _____ to see my parents and the tow truck finally arrive.

C. Complete each sentence to tell about the woods at night. What unexpected things might you see or hear? Use interesting adjectives.

13. If I were stranded in the woods at night, I might see _____
_____.

14. I might hear _____.

15. I hope I would not see _____.

16. The scariest thing would be _____.

D. (17–20) Write at least four sentences to tell about a time when you were scared. Use at least one interesting adjective in each sentence.

_____

_____

_____

_____

_____

Edit It

E. (21–25) Improve the letter. Change five adjectives to make them more interesting.

Dear Grandma,

You wouldn't believe what happened to me last night! My car died out near Wild Woods Park. It was a good thing that I had my cell phone. I called Mom right away. Mom is always so nice. She called the tow truck. My friend Maria told a bad story about a bear. Then, I started to hear noisy sounds. I thought it was a big bear. It turned out to be the wind blowing in the tree branches. I was relieved when Mom and the tow truck arrived.

Love,

Amanda

Proofreader's Marks

Change text:

The noises were ~~bad~~. spooky

See all Proofreader's Marks on page ix.

66 Can You Use an Adjective to Make a Comparison?

Yes, But You Have to Change the Adjective.

- Use a **comparative adjective** to compare two people, places, or things.

   My basketball team is **strong**, but the other team is **stronger**.
   That team is **more athletic** than ours.

- There are two ways to turn an adjective into a comparative adjective:

1. If the adjective has one syllable, add **-er**. If it has two syllables and ends in a consonant + **y**, change the **y** to i before you add **-er**.	**long** **old** **scary** **longer** **older** **scarier**
2. Use **more** before most other two-syllable adjectives. If the adjective has three or more syllables, use **more**.	**nervous** **unexpected** **more nervous** **more unexpected**

Try It

A. Complete each sentence about the opposing basketball team. Write the comparative form of the adjective.

1. Our players are **tall**, but the other players are _____.

2. We can be **intimidating**, but they are even _____.

3. Our shooting percentage is **high**, but theirs is _____.

4. Usually I am **anxious** before the game, but this time I am _____ than ever.

5. My coach is **fearful** that we will get crushed, but I am even _____.

B. Complete each sentence. Write the correct form of the adjective in parentheses.

6. The buzzer is especially _____ at the beginning of the game. **(loud)**

7. Their center is _____ than ours, and he taps the jump ball to his player. **(quick)**

8. Their second shot is _____ than their first shot. **(accurate)**

9. They score a _____ two points. **(speedy)**

10. Our defense is _____ than it should be, and we foul them on the shot. **(aggressive)**

11. They are up three to nothing, and we feel _____ now than we did before the game. **(gloomy)**

Write It

C. Compare two competing athletes, political candidates, or other celebrities. Use at least one comparative adjective in each sentence.

12. _____ is _____, but _____ is _____.

13. Right now, _____ is _____ than _____.

14. In the end, _____ will be _____ than _____.

15. I am _____ than I was _____.

D. (16–18) Write at least three sentences to compare your favorite sports team to another. Use comparative adjectives in your sentences.

_____

_____

_____

_____

_____

67 Can an Adjective Compare More Than Two Things?

Yes, But You Have to Use a Different Form.

- A **superlative adjective** compares three or more people, places, or things. You can turn an adjective into a superlative adjective:

1. Add **-est** to a one-syllable adjective or to a two-syllable adjective that ends in a consonant + **y**.	This is **the toughest** team we've ever played. They have **the pushiest** parents.
2. Use **most** before most other two-syllable adjectives. Use **most** before an adjective with three or more syllables.	They are **the most ruthless** players! It is **the most difficult** game ever.

- Use **the** before the superlative.
- Never use **more** and **-er** together. Never use **most** and **-est** together.

  It is the ~~most~~ longest game ever.

Try It

A. Write the correct adjective to complete each sentence about how the team's fear becomes a reality.

1. This game is turning into the _____ game my team has ever played.
   more humiliating/most humiliating

2. By halftime, their lead is even _____ than it was after the first quarter.
   greater/greatest

3. I feel the _____ feelings in the world.
   hopelessest/most hopeless

4. At halftime, our coach is _____, though.
   wonderful/more wonderful

5. He thinks that this is the _____ team we've ever played.
   strongest/most strongest

B. Edit the sentences. Fix the adjectives.

6. Well, my most horriblest fears have come true.

7. We have had our more terrible loss ever.

8. I am happiest after the game than I was before it, though.

9. I played my most hardest game ever.

10–11. I learned that sometimes the difficult losses of all teach us the importantest lessons.

12. I feel unhappier that we lost, but pleased that we lost by only 10 points. It could have been worse.

Write It

C. Write three new facts about the game. Use superlative adjectives in each sentence.

13. I felt the _____ of all when _____.

14. The _____ player of all the players on the other team was _____ _____.

15. The _____ moment of all the moments in the game was when _____ _____.

D. (16–20) Write an article for the school newspaper. Use at least five sentences to tell about the game. Include a comparative or superlative adjective in each sentence.

_____

_____

_____

_____

_____

_____

68 Which Adjectives Are Irregular?

Good, Bad, Many, Much, and *Little*

- Some adjectives have special forms.

To Describe 1 Thing	good	bad	many / much	few	little
To Compare 2 Things	better	worse	more	fewer	less
To Compare 3 or More Things	best	worst	most	fewest	least

- Use **many** or **few** to describe things you can count. Use **much** or **little** to describe things you can't count.

  How **many** gallons of gas did you buy?

  How **much** gas do we have now?

  There are only a **few** gas stations on this road.

  I wish we had **less** traffic and **fewer** trucks.

Try It

A. Write the correct adjective to complete each sentence.

1. I had a _____ feeling about driving down the deserted road.
   bad / worst

2. Walter had an even _____ feeling than I did.
   worse / worst

3. Fred thought that it was the _____ idea of all.
   better / best

4. So I used the _____ judgment I've ever used.
   worse / worst

5. My _____ fears of all came true.
   worse / worst

6. It was a _____ thing that I had my cell phone.
   good / better

7. Miraculously, in a _____ minutes, my mom arrived with gas.
   little / few

Write It

B. Complete the sentences to tell about when one of your fears came true. Use adjectives from the chart.

8. My _____ fear ever came true when _____

_____.

9. That experience was _____ than I thought because _____

_____.

10. Now I have the _____ memories of all because _____

_____.

C. (11–14) Write at least four sentences about fears you hope will not come true. Use adjectives from the chart on page 151.

_____

_____

_____

_____

Edit It

D. (15–18) Edit the journal entry. Fix the four incorrect adjectives.

January 15

Last night was the worst night of my life.
I made a worst decision to drive my car
with very least gas in it. It turned out to
be a bad decision than I thought. The better
thing of all the things that happened was
that Mom didn't get mad at me. She said
that she'd done some silly things when she
was a teenager, too.

Proofreader's Marks

Change text:
I had ~~most~~ more problems last
night than I expected.

See all Proofreader's Marks on page ix.

69 When Do You Use an Indefinite Adjective?

When You Can't Be Specific

- If you are not sure of the exact number or amount of something, use an **indefinite adjective**.

    The ocean has **many** sharks. **Several** kinds of sharks swim in warm water. **Some** areas have **a lot of** sharks, and **some** areas have **a few** sharks.

- Do you know which adjective to use?

These adjectives go before a noun you can count, like **sharks**:		These adjectives go before a noun you can't count, like **water**:	
many sharks	**a lot of** sharks	**much** water	**a lot of** water
a few sharks	**several** sharks	**a little** water	**not much** water
some sharks	**no** sharks	**some** water	**no** water

Try It

A. Complete each sentence with an indefinite adjective from the chart. More than one answer is possible.

1. I have _____ fear when I swim in the ocean.

2. That's because I have seen _____ movies about sharks.

3. In _____ movies, people get hurt.

4. I have _____ fear when I swim in lakes.

5. _____ sharks swim in lakes around here.

B. (6–12) Write adjectives from the chart to complete the paragraph. More than one answer is possible.

Yesterday, I was swimming _____ laps in the ocean. I was proud of

myself for overcoming _____ fears. Suddenly, I felt _____

fear because I saw _____ shark fins! My worst fears were coming

true! I felt _____ panic. Then I noticed that _____ fins were

moving. The "fins" were _____ rocks sticking up in the water.

C. Describe an ocean or a lake. Use indefinite adjectives from the chart.

13. I see _____

_____ .

14. I hear _____

_____ .

15. I enjoy _____

_____ .

16. I fear _____

_____ .

D. (17–20) Write at least four sentences about an experience you have had while you were swimming. Use indefinite adjectives.

_____

_____

_____

_____

_____

_____

Edit It

E. (21–25) Edit the report about sharks. Fix the five incorrect indefinite adjectives. There is more than one correct answer.

There are many kinds of sharks. A little sharks are dangerous. The great white shark is dangerous. Much sharks are harmless. The whale shark is harmless but huge. Much sharks have sharp teeth and eat fish. A little sharks, like the megamouth, eat plankton. Much knowledge goes a long way in understanding sharks!

Proofreader's Marks
Change text:
Many
~~Much~~ sharks live in the ^ ocean.
See all Proofreader's Marks on page ix.

70 Use Adjectives Correctly

Remember: Use adjectives to describe or compare people, places, or things.

To Describe 1 Thing	sick	uncomfortable	good	many/ much
To Compare 2 Things	sicker	more uncomfortable	better	more
To Compare 3 or More Things	sickest	most uncomfortable	best	most

I am **sick** today, but I was **sicker** yesterday. Monday was the **most uncomfortable** day of all. I am **more comfortable** today.

Try It

A. Write the correct adjective to complete each sentence.

1. I have a really _____ game on Saturday.
   big / bigger

2–3. So when I came down with the _____ sore throat in the world, I
   worse / worst
   was the _____ ever.
   more frightened / most frightened

4. I wanted to ignore it, but Mom thought it would be a _____
   better / best
   idea to go to the doctor.

5. I was _____ the doctor would say I couldn't play on Saturday.
   afraid / more afraid

6. Then my _____ fear would come true, and I would miss the game.
   horriblest / most horrible

B. Write the correct form of the adjective in parentheses.

7. It was the _____ wait ever at the doctor's office. **(long)**

8. I was even _____ than before I arrived. **(nervous)**

9. Then I heard the _____ news of all. I had strep throat. **(scary)**

10. The doctor had some _____ news than that for me, though. **(good)**

C. Complete each sentence to tell about being sick. What did you miss? Use comparative and superlative adjectives.

11. When I was sick, I felt _____.

12. That was bad, but it was even _____ when _____

_____.

13. I missed _____.

14. When I felt _____, I _____.

D. (15–18) Different things frighten different people. Write at least four sentences to tell what frightens you. Use comparative and superlative adjectives.

_____

_____

_____

_____

E. (19–25) Edit the journal entry. Fix the seven incorrect adjectives.

September 15

Today, I had the sorest throat ever. It was
the painfullest experience in the world to
swallow. I was happier to miss a day of
school, but I worried about missing the game.
In fact, I was most worried than happy.
Then, the doctor gave me the good news
ever. I had strep throat, but that wasn't the
bad thing possible. I would be best for the
game. What could have been best than that?

Proofreader's Marks

Change text:

I am ~~healthy~~ healthier now than I
was before.

See all Proofreader's Marks
on page ix.

71 Why Do You Need Adverbs?

To Tell *How, When,* **or** *Where*

- Use an **adverb** to describe a verb. Adverbs often end in **-ly**.
  The moon shines **brightly**.   (how)
  My friend and I are camping **tonight**.   (when)
  We look **up** at the sky.   (where)

- Use an **adverb** to make an adjective or another adverb stronger.
  The woods are **extremely** quiet.
                                    adjective
  Our campfire burns **very** slowly.
                          another adverb

- Adverbs add details and bring life to your writing.
  We are **really** content, and we talk **quietly**.
  Suddenly, we hear a loud shriek.

Try It

A. Write an adverb to make each sentence about the camping trip more interesting.

1. My friend and I _____ freeze.

2. We look all _____.

3. Our hearts start beating _____.

4. We feel _____ frightened.

5. Was the sound from a wild animal roaming _____?

B. (6–12) Add details with adverbs.

My imagination is _____ active under normal circumstances. Now it is
_____ working overtime. I look _____, _____, and all
around, but I see nothing. My friend and I get up _____ and run into
the tent. Then everything gets _____ quiet. We wait _____.

157

C. What happens next? Complete the sentences to tell about a frightening experience. Use an adverb in each sentence.

13. Just then, we hear _____.

14. The loud shriek _____.

15. My friend and I _____.

16. In the end, we _____.

D. (17–20) Now use your imagination. Write at least three sentences about a place that might fill you with fear. Use at least one adverb in each sentence.

_____

_____

_____

_____

_____

Edit It

E. (21–25) Add details to the conversation. Add five adverbs.

> Audrey: Our campfire is burning brightly, so it will keep animals away.
>
> Sandra: The wind is howling, so we cannot hear what might be out there.
>
> Audrey: Don't let your imagination run wild. We will wait.
>
> Sandra: Was that loud shriek an animal or a person?
>
> Audrey: I looked and didn't see anything. It's probably the wind. Let's sit.

Proofreader's Marks
Add text:
frightfully The loud noises scared Sandra.
See all Proofreader's Marks on page ix.

72 What Happens When You Add *Not* to a Sentence?

You Make the Sentence Negative.

- The word **not** is an adverb. Add **not** to a sentence to make it negative. If the verb is an **action verb**, change the sentence like this:

  Jeff **enters** the house. Jeff **does not enter** the house.

- If the verb is a form of **be**, just place **not** after the verb:

  He **is** alone. He **is not** with anyone else.

- When you shorten a verb plus **not**, replace the **o** in **not** with an apostrophe (').

1. Jeff **does not** enter the house.	**2.** He **is not** alone.
Jeff **doesn't** enter the house.	He **isn't** alone.

Try It

A. Rewrite each sentence. Add not to make it negative.

1. Jeff likes being in the big, old house. _____

_____

2. He feels safe. _____

3. The house is very quiet. _____

_____

4. Jeff concentrates on reading his book. _____

_____

5. The eerie noises are comforting to him. _____

_____

6. He wants to stay there overnight. _____

_____

7. Jeff stops his imagination from getting the best of him. _____

_____

B. Answer each question. Use **not** to write a negative sentence.

8. Is the moon shining brightly?

_____

9. Are other people in the house?

_____

10. Is the house haunted?

_____

11. Do the eerie sounds stop?

_____

12. Does Jeff run out of the scary house?

_____

13. Do people always imagine the worst when they are home alone?

_____

Write It

C. Complete each sentence about a house you live in or have visited. Use **not** to make the sentences negative.

14. The house _____.

15. I _____.

16. At night, the noises _____

_____.

D. (17–20) Write at least four negative sentences to tell about a time when your imagination ran wild and filled you with fear.

_____

_____

_____

_____

_____

73 How Do You Make a Sentence Negative?

Use One, and Only One, Negative Word.

- These words are negative words: **no**, **nobody**, **nothing**, **no one**, **not**, **never**, **nowhere**, and **none**.

- Use only one negative word in a sentence.

  Incorrect: Nobody never uses that building at night.
  Correct: Nobody ever uses that building at night.

  Incorrect: None of us could see nothing through the windows.
  Correct: None of us could see anything through the windows.

  Incorrect: We didn't have no idea who was inside.
  Correct: We didn't have any idea who was inside.
  Correct: We had no idea who was inside.

Try It

Proofreader's Marks

Delete:
I had ~~not~~ never been inside the house.

Change text:
      any
Not ~~none~~ of my friends had been inside, either.

See all Proofreader's Marks on page ix.

A. Fix each sentence to use only one negative word. There is more than one correct answer.

1. Not none of the neighbors liked having the abandoned house on the street.

2. Nobody wanted nothing to do with it.

3. At least nothing suspicious never happened there.

4. Well, not nothing happened until last night, anyway.

5. The neighbors didn't see no one going inside.

6. The house was not empty no longer, though.

7. My friends and I couldn't imagine nobody would want to live there.

8. Whoever was inside was not up to no good.

B. Rewrite each sentence to make it a negative sentence.

9. Everyone wanted to go inside the house.

_____

10. Then the police came and said all of us should go in.

_____

11. So we all waited near the house.

_____

12. When the police came out, one of them was serious.

_____

13. They did find a criminal, but they did capture a raccoon!

_____

Write It

C. Imagine you found an abandoned house. Complete each sentence to tell about your experience. Use a negative word in each sentence.

14. The old, abandoned house _____

_____.

15. I thought _____

_____.

16. At first, my imagination went wild, but then I found out _____

_____.

D. (17–20) Write a police report. Write at least four sentences about what you found in the abandoned house. Use at least four negative words.

_____

_____

_____

_____

_____

74 Can You Use an Adverb to Make a Comparison?

Yes, But You Need to Change the Adverb.

- Adverbs have different forms. Use the form that fits your purpose.

To Describe 1 Action	fast	fitfully	well	badly
To Compare 2 Actions	faster	more fitfully	better	worse
To Compare 3 or More Actions	fastest	most fitfully	best	worst

- How many things are being compared in these sentences?

    Last week, I slept the **most fitfully** that I've ever slept on a camping trip.

    I'll enjoy this camping trip **better** than I enjoyed the last camping trip.

Try It

A. Write the correct adverb to describe the action in each sentence.

1. We heard something shriek _____ than usual.

more fiercely / most fiercely

2. My imagination worked the _____ ever.

more furiously / most furiously

3. Things turned out _____ than I imagined.

more unexpectedly / most unexpectedly

4. We laughed _____ when we discovered a lost cat.

loudly / more loudly

5. This week's trip started _____ than last week's.

better / best

B. Write the correct form of the adverb in parentheses to complete each sentence.

6. Then it started to rain _____ than I've ever seen. **(fiercely)**

7. It rained the _____ of all at night. **(hard)**

8. We heard thunder roaring _____ through the woods. **(loudly)**

9. We saw lightning flashing the _____ ever. **(brightly)**

10. I waited _____ than before for the storm to end. **(desperately)**

C. Describe a rainstorm that would make your imagination work overtime. Use adverbs that compare.

11. The wind blows _____.

12. The rain falls _____.

13. Thunder roars _____.

14. Lightning flashes _____.

D. (15–19) Now imagine that you are in a tent in the woods at night. Write at least five sentences to tell what would make your imagination work overtime. Use adverbs that compare.

_____

_____

_____

_____

_____

E. (20–25) Edit the journal entry. Fix the six incorrect adverbs.

June 10

I think my camping days are over! Last week, I waited anxiously for morning because an animal was shrieking most loudly than I had heard before. Last night, I waited even anxiously for the rainstorm to end. Then the wind was blowing the more furiously ever. The thunder roared the more deafeningly ever. The lightning scared me the worse of all. I think I'll sleep happily in my own bed than in a tent!

Proofreader's Marks

Change text:

It rained ~~hard~~ harder this week than last week.

Delete:

It rained ~~more~~ harder this week than last week.

Add text:

It rained harder this week than last week.

See all Proofreader's Marks on page ix.

75 Use Adverbs Correctly

Remember: You can use adverbs to describe and compare actions. An adverb can also make another adverb or an adjective stronger.

Describe	Compare	Make Stronger
I went **hesitantly** to the scary movie.	The music blared **more frightfully** than before.	It was a **really** scary movie.
I watched **fearfully**.	I screamed the **most loudly** ever.	I was **very** scared.

Try It

A. Write adverbs to add details to the sentences.

1. I _____ like scary movies.

2. This movie was _____ scary, though.

3. The music blared the most _____ ever.

4. The special effects were _____ scary.

5. Once, I jumped _____ in my seat.

B. Complete each sentence. Write the correct form of the adverb in parentheses.

6. This movie was made from the _____ scary book of all time. **(amazingly)**

7. The movie scared me even _____ than the book did. **(badly)**

8. It seemed to be _____ suspenseful than the book. **(thoroughly)**

9. I was so _____ scared that I had to close my eyes. **(incredibly)**

10. Don't see this movie unless you want to see the _____ scary movie in the world! **(intensely)**

C. Answer the questions to tell about a scary movie you have seen. Use the correct forms of adverbs in your answers.

11. What was the most incredibly scary movie you have ever seen? _____

_____

12. Why was the movie so very scary? _____

_____

13. Which scene was the most thoroughly scary of all? What did you do when you watched

that scene? _____

_____

_____

D. (14–16) Write at least three sentences about a scary movie that triggered your imagination. Use adverbs to describe what you did and how you felt after the movie.

_____

_____

_____

_____

_____

Edit It

E. (17–20) Edit the paragraph. Fix the four incorrect adverbs.

I have the most incredibly active imagination in the world. When I am home alone, all the normally innocent-sounding house noises resonate more suspiciously like intruders. If I'm camping, every sound is a wild animal snarling most ferociously than the one before. When I'm writing a story, though, my imagination works most best. I write better rapidly when I am scared. I imagine many good ideas to write creatively about!

Proofreader's Marks

Change text:

I listen ~~most~~ *more* carefully when I'm home alone than when my family is home.

Delete:

I listen ~~more~~ better when I'm home alone than when my family is home.

See all Proofreader's Marks on page ix.

Edit and Proofread

✓ Capitalize Quotations Correctly

- Capitalize the first word of a direct quotation that is a complete sentence.

  "**How** much is the book?" asked Anil.

  The bookstore clerk replied, "**It's** $9.95, but it might be on sale."

- Do not capitalize the first word of the second part of a direct quotation when it is a continuation of the sentence.

  "I'd like to buy it," said Anil, "**if** it's on sale."

  "In that case," said the clerk, "**let** me find out for sure if it's on sale."

Try It

A. Use proofreader's marks to correct the capitalization error in each sentence.

1. "this is my favorite book," Darius said.

2. Kim asked, "why is it your favorite book?"

3. "I like it," he replied, "Because the story is suspenseful and exciting."

Proofreader's Marks
Capitalize:
The man said, "i hope you like the book." ≡
Do not capitalize:
"Yes," I said, "M̸e, too."
See all Proofreader's Marks on page ix.

B. Rewrite the following sentences as direct quotations. Be sure to use the correct capitalization. The first one is done for you.

4. He told me I should read this book because he thought I would really like it. _____ "You should read this book," he said, "because I think you will really like it."

5. I asked him who the author of the book was. _____

_____

6. He replied that Luke Samuelson was the author. _____

_____

7. I said excitedly that he was one of my favorite authors. _____

_____

✓Use Quotation Marks Correctly

- Use **quotation marks** when writing the exact words that a person said.
  Samantha said, "I'm going to the bookstore."
  "Why?" asked Andrew. "What do you need there?"

- Do not use quotation marks when describing what a person said.
  Samantha said that she needed a new book to read.

- Use a comma to set off tags, or words that identify who is quoted.
  "I'm going to go with you to the bookstore," said Andrew.
  "Hurry up," said Samantha, "because I'm leaving right now."

Try It

A. **(8–17) Add or remove quotation marks and commas where necessary. Use proofreader's marks.**

Jesse was waiting in line at the local bookstore to meet Angela Rivera, his favorite author.

I hope I can get her autograph, he muttered.

Just then, the manager said "there was only time for five more autographs." Jesse was the twelfth person in line. "I'll at least get a close look at her, he thought with disappointment."

"Young man, said a pleasant voice, why do you look so sad?"

Jesse looked up and saw Angela Rivera standing in front of him. "You're my favorite author he replied, "and I really wanted to meet you, but I was too far back in line."

"I always have time for my fans," she said. Give me your books, and I'll sign them for you."

As he left the bookstore, Jesse thought he was the luckiest person in the world.

Proofreader's Marks

Add quotation marks:
ˇCan I have the book?ˇ
she asked.

Add a comma:
"Of course you can" he
said. ⌃

Delete:
He hoped ᷉she was
happy with the book.᷉

✔Use Correct Paragraph Structure

A **paragraph** is a group of sentences that tell about the same idea. Organize sentences about the same idea into one paragraph. The **topic sentence** tells about the main, or controlling, idea of the paragraph.

Incorrect	Correct
Jan tried to put the book on the shelf, but it fell back into her bag. Then she spied the gray lady watching her. Jan's thoughts raced. What should she do or say? Carefully, Jan reached into her bag and removed the book. All the while the gray lady was watching.	**Jan tried to put the book on the shelf, but it fell back into her bag.** Then she spied the gray lady watching her. Jan's thoughts raced. What should she do or say? **Carefully, Jan reached into her bag and removed the book.** All the while the gray lady was watching.

Try It

A. **(18–20) Rewrite the story. Organize the sentences so that they follow the correct paragraph structure. You will have to make three changes.**

Cara loved to write short stories, but she was too scared to share them with anyone.

She was afraid that people would make fun of her. Then one day, Mr. Marquez gave the class an assignment to write a short story and then read it aloud to the class. Cara felt a clench in her stomach. How would she be able to stand up in front of the class and read her story?

She would have to tell Mr. Marquez that she couldn't do the assignment.

_____

_____

_____

_____

_____

_____

✓ Use Adjectives and Adverbs Correctly

- Use a **comparative adjective** to show how two things are alike or different. Add **-er** to a one-syllable adjective or to a two-syllable adjective that ends in a consonant + **y** to make it comparative. Use **more** or **less** with most other two-syllable adjectives and with adjectives of three syllables or more.

  The book I read was short, but your book was even **short<u>er</u>**.

  Which book was **more interesting**?

- Use an **adverb** to describe a verb or make an adjective or another adverb stronger. Do not use an adjective instead of an adverb. Remember that adverbs often end in **-ly**.

  My book is **really** long.
           adverb adjective

  I **quick<u>ly</u>** read it last night.
  adverb   verb

  In fact, I read it **very** quickly.
            another adverb

Try It

A. Choose the correct form of the adjective or adverb in each sentence.

21. The _____ talented young writer just published her second novel.
        amazing / amazingly

22. Critics gave her first novel rave reviews, but they think this one is even

_____.
wonderfuller / more wonderful

23. The book is _____ selling out in bookstores everywhere.
        rapid / rapidly

24. The young writer is _____ grateful for her success.
        extreme / extremely

25. She doesn't think she could be any _____ than she already is.
        luckier / more lucky

76 What's a Simple Sentence?

A Sentence with One Subject and One Predicate

You can express a complete thought with a simple sentence. In statements, the subject usually comes before the predicate.

Subject	Predicate
Our **class** noun	**studied** advertising last week. verb
Certain food **advertisements** noun	**target** teenagers. verb
The **teacher** noun	**conducted** a taste test in class. verb
The **students** noun	**tasted** three snacks and chose the best. verb

Try It

A. Identify the following phrases as a subject or predicate. Then write a complete sentence by adding the missing part.

1. Our class _____

2. tasted snacks. _____

3. The snacks _____

4. chose my favorite snack. _____

B. Add a predicate to each subject. Then underline the noun in the subject once and the verb in the predicate twice.

5. Many advertisements _____

6. People everywhere _____

7. The students _____

C. Answer the questions about an advertisement you like. Use simple sentences.

8. Which advertisements do you like? I like _____.

9. What is memorable or special about the advertisement? _____ is memorable

   because _____.

10. What does the advertisement claim about the product? _____

    _____

11. What emotions does the advertisement bring out in you? _____

    _____

D. (12–15) Write at least four simple sentences about advertisements you have seen recently.

_____

_____

_____

_____

_____

_____

Edit It

E. (16–20) Edit the advertisement. Fix the five mistakes in subjects and predicates.

> ### Hearty Oatmeal Cookies
>
> Teens need healthy snacks. love Hearty Oatmeal Cookies. Hearty Oatmeal Cookies the healthiest cookies around. They an all-natural taste just like homemade cookies. have no sugar. Everyone Hearty Oatmeal Cookies.

Proofreader's Marks
Add text: *are*   Some ads ‸ entertaining.
See all Proofreader's Marks on page ix.

77 Does the Subject Always Come First?

Not Always

In questions, the **verb** often comes before the subject.

- **Was** the taste **test** surprising?
  verb   subject

      verb . . . . verb

- **Can you predict** the most popular snack?
          subject

In some statements, the verb comes before the subject.

- Here **are** the **results** of the taste test.
         verb   subject

- **Is** this **result** ever unexpected!
    verb   subject

Try It

A. Complete each sentence about the taste test. Use the correct verb form.

1. _____ you think that people buy snacks because of the packaging?
   Do / Does

2. How _____ the class rate the unfamiliar brands?
   does / do

3. Here _____ the highest-rated snack. It is not a well-known brand.
   is / are

4. _____ this result ever a surprise!
   Was / Were

B. Put the words in the right order and write the question. Place the verb before the subject.

5. brands? / you / buy / Do / unknown _Do you buy unknown brands?_

6. less / Are / expensive? / they _____

7. they / taste / Do / good? _____

C. Answer the questions about advertising and packaging methods. Place the verb before the subject in some of your sentences.

   8. What unknown brand foods have you tried and liked? _____

   9. How did advertising influence your knowledge about the products? _____

   _____

   10. How do these products affect your opinion of unknown brands? _____

   _____

   11. What factors determine the products that people choose? For example, are commercials,

   packaging, or friends' recommendations important? _____

   _____

D. (12–15) Write at least four sentences about the advertising or packaging of a product. In one sentence, place the verb before the subject.

   _____

   _____

   _____

   _____

Edit It

E. (16–20) Edit the paragraph. For each sentence, reverse the order of subject and verb. Edits will include adding words, deleting words, changing punctuation, and capitalizing words.

Proofreader's Marks
Delete:
Does this ad ~~makes~~ make the snack tastier?
Add text:
This brand is well-known. (not)
Capitalize:
advertising affects us.
Add period:
I enjoy many snacks.
See all Proofreader's Marks on page ix.

Are unknown brands sometimes better than well-known brands? Do people tend to choose the most interesting wrapper or package? Do packaging and advertising influence our choices? Are commercials and advertisements not helpful. Never did a single commercial or wrapper tell me how a product tastes.

78 What's an Infinitive?

To + a Verb

Use **to** plus a **verb** to form an **infinitive**. An infinitive acts like a noun, an adverb, or an adjective.

- Like all nouns, an infinitive can be the **object** of an **action verb**.

  We **need to sell** more tickets. Who **wants to suggest** a strategy?
      verb   infinitive   verb   infinitive

- You can also use an infinitive in the **subject** of a sentence. The **verb** will always be singular.

  To sell tickets to the concert **is** our main goal.
  infinitive   verb

- You can also use an infinitive as an adjective or an adverb.

  Advertising **is** a way **to sell** tickets. Let's **have** a meeting **to share** ideas.
          verb   infinitive as   verb   infinitive as
                      an adjective   an adverb

Try It

A. (1–4) Complete each sentence with an infinitive.

Hemin wanted _____ flyers around our neighborhoods.

_____ our concert on the radio was Maria's idea. Another student

hoped _____ an ad in the community newspaper. We each try

_____ some tickets every day, and so far we're doing great!

B. Complete each sentence using an infinitive from the box. Write **subject**, **object**, **adjective**, or **adverb** to tell how the infinitive was used.

to advertise	to mail	to reach

5. Our gymnastics team wants _____ our competitions to boost attendance.

_____

6. We will use the student directory _____ all students. _____

7. _____ our announcements is expensive but worth it. _____

C. Answer the questions about advertising for a school-related event. Use infinitives as an object, a subject, an adjective, or an adverb.

8. How did you help to advertise an event? I helped _____.

9. To advertise effectively, what steps did you take? _____

_____

10. Who worked with you to carry out your plan? _____

11. Will you try to advertise another event in the future? Why or why not? _____

_____

D. (12–16) Write at least five sentences about effective advertising. Use infinitives in your sentences.

_____

_____

_____

_____

_____

E. (17–20) Edit the advertisement. Fix the four mistakes in infinitives.

School Musical

Please come and show your support for our theater club. To put on a musical require hard work and dedication. To perform before a full house are what our talented cast deserves. The show will take place in the high school auditorium. We hope see you there on April 22 at 8:00 p.m. We don't want you miss the best production of the year!

Proofreader's Marks

Change text:
To act ~~are~~ is a challenge.

Add text:
                      to
They hope ⌄ sell 300 tickets.

See all Proofreader's Marks on page ix.

79 Can a Verb Act Like a Noun?

Yes, When It Is a Gerund.

Add **-ing** to a **verb** to form a **gerund**. A gerund acts like a noun in a sentence.

- A gerund is often the **object** of an **action verb**.

  We **like raising** money for our school. James **loves counting** the
      verb   gerund   verb   gerund
  tickets we sell.

- You can also use a gerund as the **object** of a **preposition**.

  Summertime is a tough time **for fundraising**.
                                         gerund

- Like all nouns, a gerund is often the **subject** of a sentence.

  The **verb** will always be singular.

  Selling for fundraisers **involves** many challenges.
    gerund   verb

  Having confidence **is** important for success.
    gerund   verb

Try It

A. Complete each sentence about fundraising. Choose a verb from the box. Change it to a gerund by adding **-ing**.

ask	eat	get	hold	raise	sell

1. The fall is a good time for _____ a school fundraiser.

2. _____ funds through candy sales is usually very effective.

3. For many students, _____ people to buy the candy is difficult.

4. Sheila dislikes _____ things because she is shy.

5. Pedro dislikes _____ candy, so he has difficulty claiming that people will enjoy it.

6. _____ people to support a fundraiser is hard work!

B. Complete each sentence by changing the verb in parentheses to a gerund. Then write how it is used in the sentence, as a **subject** or an **object**, at the end of the sentence.

7. _____ a raffle ticket shows support of our school. **(buy)** _____

8. It is difficult to sell raffle tickets without _____. **(advertise)** _____

9. People like _____ raffle tickets when they know it is for a good cause. **(buy)**

_____

10. Still, _____ people to buy a raffle ticket can be difficult. **(convince)**

_____

11. I like _____ tickets, and I tend to raise a lot of money. **(sell)** _____

12. I enjoy _____ more money than anyone else in our class! **(raise)**

_____

Write It

C. Answer the questions about participating in a fundraiser. Use gerunds in your sentences.

13. Tell about a time you helped with fundraising. _____

14. What were some of the challenges of selling? _____

15. How did advertising affect your sales? _____

16. Was explaining the fundraiser easy or difficult for you? Why? _____

17. What did your experience teach you about fundraising? _____

_____

D. (18–20) Write at least three suggestions for students who plan to participate in a fundraiser. Use a gerund in each sentence.

_____

_____

_____

_____

_____

80 Vary Your Sentences

Remember: Your sentences are more interesting when you vary the word order and the types of sentences you write.

To vary your sentences, you can:

- Place a **verb** before the **subject**.
  First **comes price**. Then there **are** other **priorities** when I shop.

- Expand a sentence with an **infinitive phrase**.
  Popular labels influence some teenagers.
  Popular labels influence some teenagers **to buy products**.
                                           infinitive phrase

- Use a **gerund** or an **infinitive** as the subject of your sentence.
  Remember that these subjects always take a **singular verb**.
  To buy something just for the label **is** often expensive. **Considering**
  infinitive   gerund
  both the label and the price **shows** wisdom.

Try It

A. Rewrite each sentence. Change the underlined part to a gerund or infinitive.

1. To buy clothes is fun for my friend and me. _____

_____

2. Getting a good deal is always my priority. _____

_____

3. I do not like to spend all of my money on popular labels. _____

_____

4. My friend likes spending lots of money for popular labels. _____

_____

5. Saying who looks more stylish is difficult. _____

_____

B. (6–11) Complete each sentence with an infinitive or gerund using verbs from the box.

buy	find	get	learn	purchase	spend

_____ products is fun for my friends and me. _____ high-quality products is important. _____ too much money is not an option for me. My goal is always _____ a good sale. I try _____ the products ahead of time to learn the prices. I love _____ any product at a great price.

Write It

C. Answer the questions about shopping. Vary your sentences by including infinitives, gerunds, or verb-subject word order.

12. Do you enjoy shopping? I _____.

13. What are your priorities when buying clothes and other products? My priorities are

_____.

14. What can you do to learn about products? _____

_____

15. How do advertisements affect your decisions when buying products? _____

_____

16. Does advertising help you make a decision? If so, how? _____

_____

D. (17–20) Write at least four sentences that describe methods advertisers use to sell products. Use gerunds and infinitives.

_____

_____

_____

_____

_____

81 How Are Phrases and Clauses Different?

A Clause Has a Subject and a Predicate.

- A **phrase** is a group of words that function together. One sentence often has several phrases.

  My favorite television **series** / **shows** / a family / with teenage children.

     noun phrase   verb   noun phrase   adjective phrase

  This sentence is complete because it has a **subject** and a **verb**. A phrase never has both, so it does not express a complete thought.

- A **clause** contains a **subject** and a **verb**. An independent clause can stand alone as a sentence.

  The last **episode** **was** funny.

- **Clauses** that begin with words like **when, because,** and **if** cannot stand alone.

  When my **friends** **watch** this show

Try It

A. On the line, write one phrase from each sentence.

1. My favorite show airs on Thursday evenings. _____

2. The main characters seem like ordinary teenagers. _____

3. The parents help the teens with problems. _____

4. Their solutions work more smoothly than those in real life. _____

B. Include each phrase in a sentence about a TV game show.

5. every afternoon _____

6. the game show host _____

7. the other contestants _____

C. Answer the questions about television shows you watch. Be sure to use phrases and clauses correctly.

8. What television shows do you and your friends watch? My friends and I _____

_____.

9. Which are your favorite shows, and why? My favorite shows _____.

10. Who are your favorite characters in the shows? _____

11. How are the characters similar to and different from you? _____

_____

D. (12–14) Write at least three more sentences about television shows you like. Be sure to use phrases and clauses correctly.

_____

_____

_____

_____

E. (15–18) Edit the newspaper editorial. Fix the four mistakes to make the sentences complete.

> I support minority television channels. Growing up, I watched.
> Shows about families who are different from my own family.
> I never felt the connection my schoolmates did. When they
> talked about those shows. Then I watched. A minority channel.
> Felt instantly connected to the shows that mirror my life and
> culture.

Proofreader's Marks
Add text: many Sarai likes ⌃television shows.
Delete: The main character ⸜has interesting problems.
Do not capitalize: Television S̸hows vary widely.
See all Proofreader's Marks on page ix.

82 What's a Compound Sentence?

Two Independent Clauses Joined by *And*, *But*, or *Or*

The words **and**, **but**, and **or** are conjunctions. They join the two clauses in a **compound sentence**. A comma (**,**) comes before the conjunction.

- Use **and** to join similar ideas.

  People watch celebrities on television.
  Celebrities influence viewers in many ways.

  > **People watch celebrities on television, and celebrities influence viewers in many ways.**

- Use **but** to join different ideas.

  Some celebrities support great causes.
  People often do not learn about them.

  > **Some celebrities support great causes, but people often do not learn about them.**

- Use **or** to show a choice.

  Fans dress like their favorite musicians.
  Fans can develop their own style.

  > **Fans dress like their favorite musicians, or they can develop their own style.**

Try It

A. Combine each pair of sentences. Use **and**, **but**, or **or** to make a compound sentence.

1. Celebrities influence society. Some of them are excellent role models.

2. Some teenagers wear clothes like those of their favorite musicians. Others try to look different from everyone else.

3. People imitate the risky behaviors of some celebrities. People follow the example of celebrities who work hard.

4. Some teenagers want to look glamorous and stylish like celebrities. Others accept themselves the way they are.

5. People can buy products that celebrities advertise. They can buy products based on personal research.

Proofreader's Marks
Delete: You can wear ~~anything~~ you want.
Add a comma and text: *, and* I watch movies on TV I also watch the news. ^
Do not capitalize: Television ~~S~~hows can be interesting.
See all Proofreader's Marks on page ix.

B. **Choose the correct conjunction to combine the two related sentences.**

6. Celebrities get a lot of attention, _____ they often use it wisely.
and/or

7. Some celebrities are good role models, _____ others set a bad example.
or/but

8. My favorite celebrity supports environmental causes, _____ she
and/but
appears in an advertisement to save the rainforest.

9. Some celebrities say that they support certain causes, _____ their
or/but
actions don't reflect what they say.

10. You can choose to listen to what a celebrity says, _____ you can
and/or
make decisions based on your own research.

Write It

C. **Answer the questions below. Use compound sentences in your responses.**

11. Which television shows and magazines discuss the lives of celebrities? Which do you

like or dislike? _____ , and _____.

12. Is the information in these sources reliable? _____

13. When you hear or read about a celebrity, how can you tell if the information is true?

_____

14. How does the information affect people's opinions about celebrities? _____

_____

15. Is it fair for television and magazines to write about celebrities' families, childhoods, or

relationships? _____

D. **(16–20) Write at least four compound sentences about how celebrities are portrayed in the media and whether you think these portrayals are accurate.**

_____

_____

_____

_____

© National Geographic Learning, a part of Cengage Learning, Inc.

83 What's a Run-on Sentence?

A Sentence That Goes On and On

- To fix a run-on sentence, break it into shorter sentences.

  Run On: There are many television shows to choose from **and** I like entertainment shows **but** sometimes I also watch the news.

  Better: There are many television shows to choose from. I like entertainment shows, but sometimes I also watch the news.

- Sometimes you can also rearrange words to express the same idea.

  Run On: Local news is one kind of news show **and** national news is a different type of news show **and** so is international news.

  Better: Local, national, and international are different types of news shows.

Try It

A. Edit the three sentences that are run-ons.

1. Paula likes to watch celebrity news and I see why it interests her but I prefer to watch the national and international news.

2. I want to know about events that affect my life, and I feel news about celebrities does not impact me closely.

3. I question whether celebrity news is true and the national news seems biased sometimes but I can watch reports on different channels to check.

4. Sometimes Paula visits me and she wants to watch her favorite celebrity news channels but I watch the news as always and she usually becomes interested, too.

Proofreader's Marks

Add a period:

People are interested in celebrities⊙

Add a comma:

This news is shocking‸ but is it true?

Delete:

He likes this show, and ~~and~~ I see why.

See all Proofreader's Marks on page ix.

B. Revise each run-on sentence to make two or more shorter sentences.

5. Everyone I know prefers a different news channel and my teacher likes the international news but my parents like local news. _____

_____

6. My grandfather says that all news is biased but my father says that some channels are more biased than others and he reads the newspaper to double-check the perspective of others. _____

_____

_____

7. My teacher prefers to watch the national news and she believes it is important to keep up with politics and changes in laws and she insists that these changes always affect us. _____

_____

_____

Write It

C. Express your opinions about popular television programming by answering the following questions. Check that your answers do not include run-on sentences.

8. What types of television shows do you prefer? I prefer television shows _____

_____.

9. Why do different people like to watch different types of shows? _____

_____

10. Are television shows better for learning or for entertainment? _____

D. (11–15) Write at least five additional sentences about your opinions on television programming. Make sure not to use run-on sentences.

_____

_____

_____

_____

_____

84 How Do You Fix a Run-on Sentence?

Break It into Shorter Sentences.

- Some run-on sentences include too many phrases or clauses divided by **commas**.

  Everyone in my family has different interests, and this affects the television shows they like to watch, and this makes perfect sense, I love cooking, so I watch a cooking show almost every day.

- To fix, create shorter, more understandable sentences.

  Everyone in my family has different interests. This affects the television shows we like to watch. This makes perfect sense. I love cooking, so I watch a cooking show almost every day.

Try It

A. Fix each run-on sentence by creating shorter sentences. Punctuate each sentence correctly.

1. My family watches television after dinner and we like to watch shows together but it is difficult to agree on one channel, though.

2. My brother insists on watching game shows but I don't like game shows and my parents always want to see the news.

3. My sister reads the newspaper and news on the Internet and she doesn't want to review news again and she prefers to see reruns of her favorite comedy.

4. We all like reruns of my sister's favorite sit-com and we often watch them and we also make sure to watch a game show from time to time for my brother.

5. Sometimes I feel that we should watch the news out of respect for our parents but they watch the news anyway and they just watch it after we go to bed.

Proofreader's Marks

Delete:

The news can be informative, ~~but~~ and it can be interesting.

Capitalize:

television shows vary widely.

Add a period:

Some sit-coms are funnier than others⊙

See all Proofreader's Marks on page ix.

B. Revise these run-on sentences by forming short, understandable sentences about families and their hobbies.

6. My family members all have different interests, and my father loves to go fishing, my mother enjoys gardening, and my sister and I like listening to music. _____

_____

_____

7. One thing we do together is watch television, also we have a great system of deciding what shows to watch, and we certainly need it. _____

_____

_____

8. We watch a different show every evening, and everyone gets to choose the show at least one night every week, and if other family members don't want to watch it, they don't have to. _____

_____

_____

Write It

C. Write about your favorite forms of entertainment. Fix any run-on sentences.

9. What types of hobbies do you enjoy? I enjoy _____.

10. How does the time you spend on hobbies compare to the amount of time you watch television? I spend more time _____.

11. What time of the day do you find yourself working on different hobbies? _____

_____

D. (12–15) Write at least four sentences that tell more about your interests and hobbies. Be sure to avoid run-on sentences.

_____

_____

_____

_____

_____

85 Use Compound Sentences

Remember: A compound sentence includes two independent clauses joined by **and**, **but**, or **or**.

- Use **and** to join like ideas. Use **but** to join different ideas. Use **or** to show a choice.

    My friends and I know that television is not often realistic, **and** we want to learn about the real world. We want to visit different cultures, cities, and countries, **but** we are limited. We need to earn a lot of extra money, **or** we need to convince our parents to pay our way.

- Don't overuse **and**.

    To learn about the world, we watch video documentaries about
    different countries and cities ⊙ We ~~and~~ visiting museum exhibits on
    world cultures ⊙ Also, we ~~and~~ watching foreign films.

Try It

A. Edit the sentences. Form compound sentences by using and, but, and or when appropriate. Avoid overusing the conjunction and.

1. I ride the bus with my mother and we visit many parts of town I learn about my city.

2. My brother and I read the city paper to learn about our community and we like to look for jobs that we might want and we read about new programs for teenagers.

3. The newspaper tells about the city and many of my friends want to experience it but they cannot travel and use the Internet to research pictures. They read articles about different countries.

4. Television shows showcase different cities and cultures and sometimes they are realistic but documentaries tell more about the real world than most dramas or comedies.

Proofreader's Marks
Add a period: I like the travel channel ⊙
Add a comma: They ask the teacher and   they visit the media center.
Delete: Trains are fun, ~~and~~ but   planes are fast.
Capitalize: i like to see new places.
Add text: Check out books, read   *and*   magazines, visit Web sites.
See all Proofreader's Marks on page ix.

B. Form correct compound sentences about ways television affects our view of the world. Use **and**, **but**, and **or** when appropriate. Avoid overusing the conjunction **and**.

5. Television makes the world look brighter than it is. The real world is not as beautiful as the one on TV. _____

_____

6. Houses in shows are perfectly clean. Outside settings look unnaturally beautiful. _____

_____

7. Television sometimes shows the world as simple. Problems in the real world are not that simple. _____

_____

8. My friends want to know about real life in other countries. They want to learn about other cultures. _____

_____

Write It

C. Answer the questions about differences you have noticed between real life and television. Use compound sentences correctly in your answers.

9. How do people on television look and act differently from people in real life? People on TV _____.

10. How do images on television affect people's feelings about real life? _____

_____.

11. How do images on television relate to real life? _____

_____.

D. (12–15) Write at least four more compound sentences about ways that television relates to real life. Avoid overusing the conjunction **and**.

_____

_____

_____

_____

86 What's a Complex Sentence?

A Sentence with Two Kinds of Clauses

- A clause has a **subject** and a **verb**. An **independent clause** can stand alone as a sentence.

  I saw a protest.
  <u>independent clause</u>

- A **dependent clause** also has a subject and a verb. But it cannot stand alone.

  when my **family went** downtown
  <u>dependent clause</u>

- You can "hook" the dependent clause to an independent clause to form a complete sentence. The new sentence is called a **complex sentence**.

  I saw a protest when my **family went** downtown.
  <u>independent clause</u>   <u>dependent clause</u>

Try It

A. Form complex sentences about news coverage. Draw a line to connect each independent clause with a dependent clause.

1. We saw about one hundred protesters

   because it claimed that there were "several" marchers who "behaved badly."

2. We parked close to the protest

   when we were driving.

3. The people remained calm and orderly

   as they marched silently to protest their wages.

4. The next morning we read about the march in the newspaper

   because we wanted to read the signs.

5. We were surprised by the article

   as we ate breakfast.

6. The article exaggerated

   because most people were well behaved.

B. Write whether each clause is independent or dependent. If dependent, rewrite it to create a complex sentence. If independent, punctuate it correctly to form a sentence.

7. the media can shape people's impressions _____

_____

8. when an incident took place recently at the football game _____

_____

9. but a few fans argued _____

_____

10. a reporter wrote about it _____

Write It

C. Answer the questions about media coverage of events. Use complex sentences.

11. What incident do you know about that the media reported with bias? I know that

_____.

12. How do you think the reports affected people's perceptions? _____

13. What did this event and its coverage teach you about the media? _____

14. If events are reported with bias, how can you learn the truth about what you read?

_____

15. When you detect bias in a source, do you continue to read it? Why or why not?

_____

D. (16–20) Write at least five sentences about bias in media reporting.
Include complex sentences in your responses.

_____

_____

_____

_____

_____

_____

87 Can a Clause Act Like an Adverb?

Yes, and It Often Tells When or Why.

- A **complex sentence** has one independent clause and one dependent clause.

  Newspapers include photographs **because they help readers understand events.**

  independent clause   dependent clause

- When the **dependent clause** acts like an adverb, it begins with a **subordinating conjunction**. The conjunction shows how the two clauses are related.

Tells When:	**After** I came home from school, I flipped through a magazine.
Tells Why:	**Since** I took exams all day, I now want to read for enjoyment.
Tells What May Happen:	I will read any article **if it has an interesting photo**.

- More **conjunctions** include: before, when, whenever, while, until, because, unless, although.

Try It

A. Create complex sentences about photographs that illustrate news articles. Add a clause that begins with a subordinating conjunction.

1. I read the article about the game _____

   _____

2. _____, the photograph conveyed

   additional details, such as the emotions of the players.

3. I let my friend borrow the newspaper _____.

4. _____, we talked about parts of the game.

5. We didn't remember how exciting it was _____.

B. Complete each complex sentence with a subordinating conjunction that tells **when, why,** or **what may happen.**

6. Kristin wrote an article about our graduation _____ it took place. **(when)**

7. I gave her photographs of the ceremony to clip to the article _____ she sent the article to the newspaper. **(when)**

8. She chose the photograph of the class cheering together _____ their faces communicated their mood. **(why)**

9. She will send the photograph with the article _____ they may not publish it. **(what may happen)**

Write It

C. Answer the questions below about ways photographs reveal truth or create bias. Use complex sentences with clauses that act as adverbs.

10. Describe photographs you have seen that revealed the truth about people or events.
I have seen _____.

11. Have you seen photographs that disguised the truth or created bias? Describe them.
_____

12. In which periodicals have you noticed enhanced photographs of people or places?
_____

D. (13–15) Write at least three sentences to tell more about ways photographs reveal or disguise the truth. Use complex sentences with clauses that act as adverbs.

_____

_____

_____

_____

_____

88 Can a Clause Act Like an Adjective?

Yes, and It Often Begins with *Who*, *That*, or *Which*.

- A **complex sentence** has one independent clause and one dependent clause.
  Students read school newspapers **that contain sensationalized articles.**

  <u>independent clause</u>   <u>dependent clause</u>

- Some **dependent clauses** act like adjectives and tell more about a noun.
  They begin with a **relative pronoun**.
  1. Use **who** to tell about a person.
  2. Use **that** for things or people.
  3. Use **which** for things.

- Place an **adjective clause** right after the noun it describes.

  I prefer <u>newspapers</u> **that contain plain and simple facts**.

  I know many other <u>students</u> **who agree with me**.

  I write for the *North High News*, **which comes out once a month**.

Try It

A. Complete each sentence by adding the relative pronoun who or that.

1. Students always discuss the articles _____ are sensationalized.

2. They don't want to write for newspapers _____ contain exaggerations.

3. I know others _____ think that will make the newspaper boring.

4. The editors will not approve a change _____ will make the paper boring.

B. Read the sentences about newspaper articles. Add an adjective clause to each.

5. My parents say many newspapers contain articles _____

   _____.

6. All of the students _____ know why.

7. Our old school newspaper, _____, includes some sensational details.

C. Answer the questions about sensationalized news. Use relative pronouns that introduce adjective clauses.

8. Describe one periodical in which you have read sensationalized news. I have read the

periodical _____, which _____.

9. How do you feel about the information in this source? I feel _____.

10. How do you know when an article is sensationalized? _____

11. Do you feel that sensationalizing media is dishonest or necessary? Why? _____

_____

D. (12–15) Write at least four additional sentences about your feelings about sensationalized media. Use adjective clauses in your responses.

_____

_____

_____

_____

Edit It

E. (16–20) Edit the ad. Fix the five mistakes with relative pronouns.

We have made a toothpaste that will change your life! It has a taste who makes people leap out of bed every morning. People which feel that brushing their teeth is a boring chore will change their minds. Once you use a toothpaste who sparkles and glows like this one, you will never change brands. People which use our toothpaste claim it whitens their teeth! Don't wait to try something who will change your life.

Proofreader's Marks

Change text:

People ~~which~~ who read this magazine like exciting news.

See all Proofreader's Marks on page ix.

(89) Can a Clause Act Like a Noun?

Yes, and It Can Substitute for a Noun Any Place in a Sentence.

- A clause can function like a noun in a sentence. The <u>noun clause</u> can begin with **that,** or a *wh-* word such as **why, what,** or **when.**

  <u>**What** our founders wrote</u> laid the foundation for our society.
       subject

  The Declaration of Independence explains <u>**why** everyone should be considered equal.</u>
       direct object

  Mr. Kim says it should be required reading for <u>**whoever** runs for office.</u>
       object of the preposition *for*

- When there is more than one noun clause, use parallel structure.

  Mr. Kim claims <u>**that** the document is as important as the Constitution,</u> <u>**that** every student should study it,</u> and <u>**that** we should all memorize it.</u>

Try It

A. Underline the noun clauses. Which sentence has parallel structure?

1. I understand why the Declaration of Independence is so important.

2. It states that all men are created equal, that they are endowed by their creator with certain unalienable rights, and that among these are life, liberty, and the pursuit of happiness.

3. What they meant by "men" is not clear.

4. I believe that they used the word "men" to mean both genders.

5. The meaning must be considered by whoever reads the document.

B. Add a word to complete each noun clause. Then tell how it functions in the sentence.

6. I believe _____ Americans will always value *The Declaration of Independence*.

7. _____ value it has varies among people.

8. That may explain _____ people interpret it differently.

9. Our founders claimed _____ all men deserve life, liberty, and the pursuit of happiness.

10. I claim _____ "men" includes all of us.

11. Some people might argue about _____ the word "men" means.

12. _____ some prejudiced person says will not change my mind.

Write It

C. Read the sentences. Add a noun clause to each.

13. I predict _____.

14. A talk-show host on TV claims _____

_____.

15. _____ is not important to me.

D. (16–18) Write three sentences about how people disagree. Use a noun clause in each sentence. Begin each noun clause with *that*, or a *wh-* word such as *why, what,* or *whoever.* Use parallel structure in one sentence.

_____

_____

_____

_____

_____

_____

90 Use Complex Sentences

Remember: Sentence variety adds interest to your writing.

Expand a simple sentence to a **complex sentence**.

- Add an **adjective clause** to tell more about a noun.
  Use a **relative pronoun** (that, which, who).

  I read the article about genes.

  I read the article about genes, **which is what I want to study in college**.

- Replace a noun with a **noun clause**.
  People argue about **how ethical gene manipulation is**.

- Add an **adverb clause** to tell more about an action.
  Use a **subordinating conjunction** (after, although, if, because).
  People check sources on the Internet **if they want the most current information**.

Try It

A. Revise each sentence by adding an adjective or adverb clause. Write **adjective** or **adverb** on the line.

1. Newspapers contain information. _____

   _____.

2. Web sites stay even more current. _____

   _____.

3. Many teenagers have phones. _____

   _____.

4. Almost everyone gets news from the Web. _____

   _____.

5. Some teenagers check news updates on their phones. _____

   _____

   _____.

B. Use each noun clause below in a sentence.

6. what we read on the Internet _____
   _____

7. where we get information _____
   _____

8. what I was looking for _____
   _____

C. Answer the questions about the ways you prefer to receive information. Vary your sentences by using adjective, adverb, and noun clauses.

9. What are some ways you like to receive information? I like to receive information _____ because _____.

10. Why do you like these ways best? I like these ways best _____.

11. What do these methods reveal about your personality and priorities? _____

12. What are your favorite sources of information? _____

13. What are ways to receive information that you would like to explore? _____
    _____

D. (14–18) Write at least five more sentences that describe ways you prefer to receive information. Vary your sentences by making them complex.

_____
_____
_____
_____
_____
_____

✓ Capitalize Specific School Courses

- Capitalize the names of courses in school only when they are languages or names of specific courses.

  Are you taking **Spanish** next year?

  I am signed up for **Algebra I**.

- Do not capitalize general course names.

  Melanie uses skills from her **art** class at her after-school job.

  Brett needs to finish his **geometry** homework before basketball practice.

Try It

A. (1–5) Fix the five capitalization errors in the letter. Use proofreader's marks.

Dear Mr. Menendez:

I am writing to apply for a summer job with your construction company. I am very interested in studying Architecture in college, and I think working for you would be a great experience. I have no problem getting to work early in the morning because I've been waking up before sunrise to do observations for my Astronomy class. I am also familiar with basic construction principles because I've taken several Engineering courses, including introductory AutoCAD and advanced Autodesk Inventor 3D. I promise you that I am a hard worker and will make the most of the experience.

Sincerely,

Faith Jackson

Proofreader's Marks

Capitalize:

I need help with my french homework.

Do not capitalize:

I can help you study for your Physics test.

See all Proofreader's Marks on page ix.

B. (6–7) Write at least two sentences about general and specific courses you would like to take at your school. Be sure to use correct rules of capitalization.

_____

_____

Use Semicolons and Commas Correctly

- Use a **semicolon** to join two complete sentences that are related. If a word like **however** or **therefore** links two sentences, use a semicolon before the word and a comma after it.

    Omar works after school; he's a bagger at the supermarket.

    Sierra doesn't want to get a job; **however,** she needs to earn some money.

- Use a **comma** with a **coordinating conjunction** to join two complete sentences.

    Jessica works at the mall during the week, **and** she is a lifeguard on weekends.

    Derek wants an after-school job, **but** he has football practice every day until 6:00.

    Andrea can get a job as a waitress, **or** she can volunteer at a nursing home.

Coordinating Conjunctions
and (to join like ideas)
but (to join different ideas)
or (to show a choice)

Try It

A. Edit each sentence. Add a semicolon and/or a comma where necessary. Use proofreader's marks.

8. The new clothing store in town is hiring the managers are looking for high school students to work part-time.

9. Maya and I are walking downtown after school and we're going to fill out applications.

10. I would go with you however I have soccer practice.

11. You can go tomorrow or you can go on Saturday morning.

12. I would go on Saturday morning but I have a soccer game.

B. (13–14) Write at least two sentences about your after-school job or activities. Be sure to use correct punctuation in each sentence.

_____

_____

Proofreader's Marks
Add a semicolon:
I have no money˄ therefore˄ need to get a job.
Add a comma:
I'd like to work on weekdays˄but I'd prefer not to work on weekends.

✔ Use Precise Language

- Substitute general words with specific words.

  I got a job at a store.

  I got a job at **the local hardware store**.

- Replace words such as **few**, **many**, and **some** with specific amounts.

  I can earn some money every week.

  I can earn fifty dollars every week.

- Add a word or phrase to provide more information about another word.

  I perform many different tasks.

  I perform **many different tasks, such as helping customers, working the cash register, and stocking shelves**.

Try It

A. Rewrite each sentence. Replace the underlined word or phrase with more precise language or add more precise language to describe it.

15. Raul needs <u>some money</u>.

_____

16. He is saving up for <u>something</u>.

_____

17. He wants to apply for <u>a job</u>.

_____

18. Mrs. Turner needs <u>some extra help</u>.

_____

19. She wants to hire someone who can work <u>many hours</u>.

_____

20. She needs someone with <u>a lot of experience</u>.

_____

✔ Build Effective Sentences

- When joining two sentences with a **subordinating conjunction**, make sure the conjunction goes with the less important sentence. That way, the less important sentence supports the main sentence instead of the opposite.

Subordinating Conjunctions
before, when (to show time)
because, so (to show cause and effect)
although, even though (to show opposition)

    Incorrect: Even though I never have enough money, I have a job.

    Correct: Even though I have a job, I never have enough money.

- When combining sentences, keep elements of the new sentence parallel in form. This means they should have the same grammar form.

    Incorrect: Sam enjoys **meeting** new people and **to stock** shelves.

    Correct: Sam enjoys **meeting** new people and **stocking** shelves.

Try It

A. Rewrite each sentence. Correct the placement of the subordinating conjunction, or make the sentence parts parallel.

21. They didn't get enough sleep because they are tired.

_____

22. Although I get only seven hours of sleep, I need eight.

_____

23. A lack of sleep can cause depression and being careless.

_____

24. When you sleep enough, you feel alert and have high energy.

_____

25. Poor sleep results in lower grades and scoring low on tests.

_____

91 Why Do Verbs Have So Many Forms?

Because They Change to Show When an Action Happens

The tense of a verb shows when an action happens.

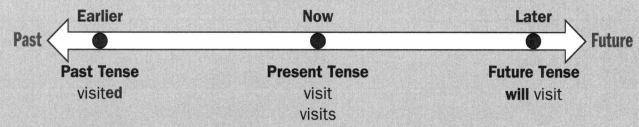

- **Present tense** verbs tell about actions that happen now or on a regular basis.

    I **visit** my grandparents. I always **go** to their house.

- **Past tense** verbs tell about actions that already happened. Add **-ed** to show the past, or use the correct form of an irregular verb.

    I **visited** my grandparents a year ago. I **went** to their house last July.

Present Tense	am, is	are	have, has	go, goes	see, sees
Past Tense	was	were	had	went	saw

- **Future tense** verbs tell about actions that haven't happened yet.

    I **will visit** my grandparents soon. I **will go** to their house next week.

Try It

A. Rewrite each sentence. Change the underlined verb to the past tense.

1. My family <u>lives</u> here. We <u>like</u> this neighborhood. _____

_____

2. I <u>see</u> my grandmother every day. She <u>helps</u> me with my homework. _____

_____

3. I <u>am</u> happy to live near her. We <u>have</u> a lot of fun together. _____

_____

B. Complete each sentence with a verb from the box. Use the correct tense of the verb: past, present, or future. You can use words more than once.

are	call	come	live	miss	move	stay	visit

4. Last year, my family _____ to New York.

5. My father _____ here because of a new job.

6. When we left, my grandparents _____ in the Philippines.

7. My sisters and I _____ very sad the day we left.

8. Now, we _____ very far from our grandparents.

9–10. A year ago, we _____ next door to them. I still _____ them.

11–12. They _____ us every weekend. Next summer, we _____ them.

Write It

C. Answer the questions about moving to a new place. Use past, present, and future tense verbs.

13. Who in your family has moved to a new community? _____

14. Is it difficult to be separated from family members? _____

15. How can you stay in touch with family members? _____

16. Tell about a visit to family members that you have made or might make in the future.

_____

_____

D. (17–20) Write at least four sentences to tell more about family members who live far away. Use past, present, and future tense verbs.

_____

_____

_____

_____

_____

92 What If an Action Happened But You're Not Sure When?

Use the Present Perfect Tense to Tell About It.

- If you know when an action happened in the past, use a **past tense** verb.
  Last month, my older brother **traveled** twice for job interviews.

- If you're not sure when a past action happened, use
  a verb in the **present perfect tense**.
  Jeffrey **has traveled** for interviews many times.

- To form the present perfect, use the helping verb **have** or **has** plus the **past participle** of the main verb. For regular verbs, the past participle ends in -**ed**.

Verb	Past Tense	Past Participle
like	liked	liked
shop	shopped	shopped
try	tried	tried

Try It

A. Complete each sentence. Use the past tense or the present perfect tense.

1. Three months ago, Jeffrey _____ away.
  moved / has moved

2. Just before he left, he _____ a job in another city.
  accepted / has accepted

3. We _____ to visit him every week.
  tried / have tried

4. The first time we went, I _____ his apartment.
  liked / have liked

5. Last Thursday, Mary Jane _____ to join us.
  decided / has decided

6. She _____ Jeffrey many times before.
  visited / has visited

B. Write the correct past tense or present perfect tense of the verb in parentheses.

7. Over the past month, my parents _____ their work schedules. **(change)**

8. Yesterday, my father _____ until nine o'clock. **(work)**

9. He _____ us several times that his company is expanding. **(tell)**

10. Last week, my mother's boss _____ her to work on Saturdays. **(ask)**

11. My mother _____ to his request a few times. **(agree)**

12. Over time, I _____ to their new schedules. **(adjust)**

13. Last night, I _____ for groceries to help out. **(shop)**

14. Then I _____ my homework. **(finish)**

15. For the past few weeks, we _____ to make the best of the situation. **(try)**

Write It

C. Answer the questions about yourself and a recent change in your family. Use past tense and present perfect tense verbs in your sentences.

16. In the last year, what change has occurred in your family? In the last year, _____
_____
_____.

17. What effect has that change had on you? _____
_____
_____.

D. (18–20) Write at least three sentences to tell more about the change in your family. Use past tense and present perfect tense verbs in your sentences.

_____
_____
_____
_____

93 What If a Past Action Is Still Going On?

Then Use the Present Perfect Tense.

- Use the **present perfect tense** to show that an action began in the past and may still be happening.

    Our family **has created** a very successful business.
    (And we are still running this business.)
    We **have enjoyed** our success. (And we are still enjoying our success.)

Past   Earlier   Now   Later   Future

Present Perfect Tense
has created **have** enjoyed

- A verb in the present perfect tense uses the helping verb **have** or **has** plus the **past participle** of the main verb. For regular verbs, the past participle ends in **-ed**.

Try It

A. (1–5) Write a verb to complete each sentence. Use the present perfect form of the verb in parentheses.

My relatives _____ as builders for years. **(work)** We

_____ a reputation for good craftsmanship. **(earn)** Sometimes, my

uncles _____ about the business. **(argue)** Then they _____

on a plan. **(agree)** Our business _____ even through tough times. **(last)**

B. Rewrite each sentence to tell about something that happened in the past. Use the present perfect tense.

6. Uncle Leo and I review the architect's drawings.

_____

7. We discuss the work schedule.

_____

8. We consult with the building inspector.

_____

C. Answer the questions about a business or project that you and your family have worked on together. Use the present perfect tense in some of your sentences.

9. What is a business or project that you have worked on with your family? My family

_____

_____.

10. Did you enjoy working with your family? _____

_____

D. (11–14) Write at least four sentences to tell more about a family business or project. Use the present perfect tense in some of your sentences.

_____

_____

_____

_____

_____

E. (15–20) Edit the brochure below. Fix the six mistakes by using the present perfect tense of verbs.

Milbane Motor Company has existed as a family-run car dealership for fifty years. We has focus on providing our customers great cars at low prices. We has helped thousands of people find the car of their dreams. Our family has work hard to build a business you can trust. We enjoy serving the downtown area for many years. We add many used cars to our lot. Tim, Paul, and Rita Milbane invite you to visit our showroom today and see what we accomplish over the past five decades.

Proofreader's Marks
Change text:
have earned
We ~~earn~~ our good reputation over the years.
See all Proofreader's Marks on page ix.

94 Do All Past Participles End in -ed?

No, Irregular Verbs Have Special Forms.

- Past participles of irregular verbs have completely new spellings.

	Verb	Past Tense	Past Participle
Forms of Be	am, is	was	been
	are	were	been
	give	gave	given
	go	went	gone
	see	saw	seen

- Use **has** or **have** plus the past participle to form the **present perfect tense**.

    My family **has seen** how frail our grandmother has become.

    My parents **have been** very worried about her.

Try It

A. Complete each sentence. Write the present perfect form of the verb in parentheses.

1. My mother _____ to take care of my grandmother. **(go)**

2. My grandmother _____ sick. **(is)**

3. I _____ my grandmother only once this year. **(see)**

4. She _____ us many treasures. **(give)**

B. (5–8) Add an irregular verb in the present perfect form to complete each sentence.

My sisters and I _____ waiting for good news. My father _____ to help my mother. They _____ my grandmother medicine every four hours. My parents say that this week _____ hard for them.

C. Answer the questions about different generations of a family helping each other. Use irregular verbs in some of your sentences.

9. How have different generations of your family helped each other? _____

_____

10. What have you done to help if a parent or grandparent is ill? _____

_____

11. What other kinds of help have you given to parents or grandparents? _____

_____

D. (12–15) Write at least three sentences about how your relatives have helped each other. Use irregular verbs in the present perfect tense in some of your sentences.

_____

_____

_____

_____

_____

Edit It

E. (16–20) Edit the letter below. Fix the five mistakes. Use the present perfect tense of the verbs.

Dear Aunt Tanya,

 Ben and I have been eager to share news about our baby cousin. We have went to visit him three times. Kevin been such a good baby. We has see him every day. I has give him his bottle twice! Ben is be even more excited than I have!

Your loving niece,

Janet

Proofreader's Marks
Add text: She $\overset{has}{\wedge}$ given him a bottle.
Change text: We $\underset{\wedge}{\overset{have}{has}}$ seen the baby.
See all Proofreader's Marks on page ix.

95 Verbs in the Present Perfect Tense

Remember: Use **have** or **has** plus the past participle of a verb to form the present perfect tense.

- The past participle of a **regular verb** ends in **-ed**.
  My sister **has act<u>ed</u>** rudely towards everyone in our family. **(act + -ed)**
  My parents **have arrang<u>ed</u>** for a family meeting. **(arrange [− e] + -ed)**
- The past participle of an **irregular verb** has a completely new spelling.

Verb	Past Participle		Verb	Past Participle
be	been		hold	held
come	come		show	shown
get	got or gotten		take	taken

Try It

A. Complete each sentence. Use the present perfect tense of the verb in parentheses.

1. My sister _____ more irritable recently. **(seem)**

2. I _____ upset by her behavior. **(be)**

3. My parents _____ more patience. **(show)**

4. My sister _____ clothes from my room. **(take)**

5. My mother _____ home early to talk with her about it. **(come)**

6. I _____ my temper as long as I can. **(hold)**

B. Add a verb in the present perfect form to complete each sentence.

7. For many years, we _____ very close.

8. Lately, my sister _____ me badly.

9. More recently, she _____ that she wants to improve our relationship.

C. Answer the questions about conflicts. Use the present perfect tense.

10. What has been the cause of a conflict between you and a sibling or parent? _____

_____

11. How have you resolved this conflict? _____

_____

12. What advice has someone given you about how to deal with conflicts? _____

_____

D. (13–15) Write at least three sentences to tell more about how you have handled conflict with a family member. Use the present perfect tense.

_____

_____

_____

_____

_____

_____

Edit It

E. (16–20) Edit the journal entry. Fix the five mistakes.

> March 12
>
> Recently, I have been upset with my father.
> We has argue constantly about his rules. I
> have show him that I am responsible. Even my
> brothers taken my side in the argument. My
> friends has got tired of me having to be
> home so early. They can stay out later. Until
> recently, I has been so close to my father. I
> hope we can find a way to resolve this soon.

Proofreader's Marks

Add text:
We ⌃ gone.   *have*

Change text:
I ~~has~~ ⌃ been angry.   *have*

See all Proofreader's Marks on page ix.

96 How Do You Show Which Past Action Happened First?

Use the Past Perfect Tense.

- Use the **past tense** of a verb to tell about an action that was completed in the past.
  Last week, I **missed** going to the game.

- If you want to show that one past action happened before another, use the
  past perfect tense for the action that happened first.
  I **had planned** to go before my parents **asked** me to help.

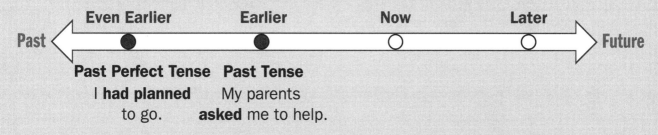

Even Earlier	Earlier	Now	Later

Past ← ● ● ○ ○ → Future

Past Perfect Tense   **Past Tense**
I **had planned**   My parents
     to go.   **asked** me to help.

- To form the **past perfect tense**, use **had** plus the **past participle** of the main verb.
  I **told** them I would help although I **had wanted** to see the game.

Try It

A. Write the past perfect tense of the verb in parentheses.

1. I _____ Lauren that I would go before I agreed to help my parents. **(assure)**

2. Lauren called me at 6 P.M., but I _____ the job. **(start)**

3. I _____ Lauren to go anyway, but she came over to help. **(tell)**

4. We _____ the job before the game was even over. **(finish)**

B. Complete each sentence by using the past perfect tense.

5. I felt grateful that Lauren _____ me.

6. Lauren said she _____ to spend time with me.

7. I said I _____ being with her, too.

C. Answer the questions about helping friends. Use the past perfect tense.

8. Have you ever given up going to an important event to help a friend? Explain. I _____

_____.

9. How has a friend helped you? _____

10. How has your friend's actions influenced your feelings about the friendship? _____

_____

D. (11–15) Write at least five sentences to tell more about helping or being helped by a friend. Use the past perfect tense.

_____

_____

_____

_____

_____

Edit It

E. (16–20) Edit the journal entry. Fix the five mistakes.

January 23

I had been really nervous about my oral
report before Max help me. On Tuesday, I
asked him if I could practice reading my report
aloud to him. Before I talk to him, he had
arrange to go skating. He changed his plans
and listened to me read. After I have practice
in front of Max, he said the report was good.
Though I had be nervous at first, with his help,
I was calm when I presented my report in class.

Proofreader's Marks

Change text:
                    hoped
I had ~~hope~~ to practice.

See all Proofreader's Marks
on page ix.

ⓐ How Do You Know Which Tense to Use?

Think About When the Action Happened.

- When you tell about the past, you may need to relate actions in time. First use the **past tense** to tell what happened.

    Yesterday, Jamil and Juan **had** a heated discussion about baseball.

- Then use the **past perfect tense** to tell what happened before the discussion.

    They **had discussed** sports often.

- Sometimes a past action may still be going on. That's when you use the **present perfect tense**.

    Jamil and Juan **have disagreed** about sports before.

    They **have attended** many games together since they first **met**.

Try It

A. Complete each sentence. Use the correct form of the verb.

1. Jamil knew Juan from school, but he _____ him from the

                                      knew / had known

   neighborhood first.

2. At school, they had many other friends, although they _____

                                          were / have been

   best friends for many years.

3. Juan played baseball like Jamil, but recently he _____ that

                                 has realized / had realized

   soccer is more fun for him.

4. Last Friday, Jamil noticed that Juan _____ to sit with the

                                 chose / had chosen

   soccer team at lunch.

5. Today, Jamil _____ Juan whether he was still mad about their

                     asked / had asked

   recent argument.

6. Juan explained that he _____ to introduce himself to the soccer team.

                 has wanted / had wanted

    217

B. Write the correct tense of the verb in parentheses. Use the past, past perfect, or present perfect tense.

7. Ann and I talked about how we _____ in math class. **(met)**

8. Last year, Ann _____ to my town. **(move)**

9. Before that, she _____ in another state. **(live)**

10. Our math teacher _____ us into groups to study for a test. **(divide)**

11. Ann and I _____ in the same group. **(be)**

12. I thought math was hard, but Ann _____ math since she was little. **(like)**

13. She made math interesting, and we _____ friends ever since. **(be)**

14. We _____ lots of time together since we met in that group. **(spend)**

Write It

C. Answer the questions about yourself and a good friend. Use verbs in the past, past perfect, and present perfect tenses.

15. Think of a good friend. How did you meet that person? I _____
_____.

16. Did you become friends right away or did it take time? Explain. _____
_____

17. What interests or activities have you shared with this friend? _____
_____

D. (18–20) Write at least three sentences to tell more about how you met or got to know your friend.

_____
_____
_____
_____

98 When Do You Use the Future Perfect Tense?

When You Want to Relate a Future Action to a Future Time

- Sometimes an action that hasn't yet happened depends on another future event. That's when you use the **future perfect tense**.

  Soon **summer will be here**. By then, I **will have finished** my junior year.

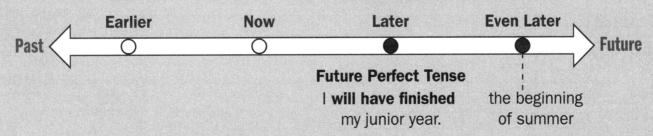

- To form the **future perfect tense**, use **will have** plus the **past participle** of the main verb.

  Before summer comes, I **will have joined** the gymnastics team.

  By next week, Eduardo **will have started** practicing with the swim team.

Try It

A. Complete each sentence. Use the future perfect form of the verb in parentheses.

1. This summer, I _____ friends with Eduardo for five years. **(be)**

2. By next year, we _____ to school together for three years. **(go)**

3. We _____ different school teams by the fall. **(join)**

4. Hopefully, by the end of summer, we _____ friends. **(stay)**

5. Before the summer ends, we _____ some time together. **(enjoy)**

B. Rewrite each sentence to tell about something in the future. Use the future perfect tense.

6. Eduardo and I watch the movie. _____

_____

7. We laugh at the funny parts together. _____

_____

8. Tony sees a different movie. _____

C. Answer the questions about yourself and your friends. Use the future perfect tense.

9. How do you think your friendships might change in the future? In the future, I _____

_____.

10. What events might change a friendship? _____

_____

11. What will you and your friends have done by the end of the school year? _____

_____

D. (12–15) Write at least four sentences about yourself and one or more of your friends. Tell what you think will happen in the future.

_____

_____

_____

_____

_____

E. (16–20) Edit the letter. Fix the five mistakes. Use the future perfect tense of the verbs.

Dear Uncle Hector,

By next Wednesday, I will have competed in the swim meet. Hopefully, before the meet is over, I got a medal. By the following week, I has start rehearsals for my band concert. By the time the concert night arrives, I rehearsed for about 20 hours. Also, I miss a party that's happening that same night. I am so busy, I don't have much time to spend with my friends. But I hope that by the time you read this, I have some time to relax with my family.

Your nephew,

Julio

Proofreader's Marks

Change text:
will have finished
I has~~ finish~~ my work.

See all Proofreader's Marks on page ix.

99 How Are the Past Perfect and Future Perfect Tenses Alike?

They Both Show How One Action Happens Before Another.

- Use the **past perfect tense** to help your readers know that an action happened even earlier than another past action.

    Before the school year **ended**, I **had transferred** to a new school.

- Use the **future perfect tense** to help your readers know that an action will happen before some other time in the future.

    By the time summer comes, I **will have made** lots of new friends.

Try It

A. Complete each sentence. Use the past perfect or future perfect tense of the verb in parentheses.

1. Before our school closed, I _____ many friends. **(make)**

2. When I left the building, I _____ good-bye to everyone. **(say)**

3. By next fall, I _____ a new school in a new neighborhood. **(enter)**

4. By the time I join a team, I _____ some new classmates. **(meet)**

B. Add a verb in the past perfect or future perfect tense to complete each sentence.

5. At my old school, I _____ many teachers.

6. After the first day at my new school, I _____ other teachers.

7. After the first semester, I _____ more comfortable at the new school.

8. Before I changed schools, I _____ to play soccer.

9. By the end of next year, I _____ with a new coach.

Write It

C. Answer the questions about yourself and changes you have or will have experienced. Use verbs in the past perfect or future perfect tense in your sentences.

10. What would happen to your friendships if you had to change schools? _____

_____

11. Describe how a student makes new friends after transferring to a different school.

_____

_____

D. (12–15) Write at least four sentences about what you might do at a new school or what you did at an old school. Use verbs in the past perfect or future perfect tense in your sentences.

_____

_____

_____

_____

_____

Edit It

E. (16–20) Edit the letter. Fix the five mistakes with verbs. Use the past, past perfect, or future perfect tense of the verbs.

Dear Isabella,

By the time you read this, I will have finished the fall semester at school. Before Thanksgiving, my parents have a place for us to live in Chicago. Soon, Nancy and I say good-bye to our neighborhood friends. Last week, we pack up lots of household items to donate to a local thrift store. By the time we were done, I will have gotten rid of my old bike. Before we are all moved in, Dad says he buys me a new one!

Your friend,

Carlos

Proofreader's Marks

Change text:
We ~~will pack~~ will have packed all our books.

See all Proofreader's Marks on page ix.

(100) Write with the Perfect Tenses

Remember: Use the present perfect, past perfect, and future perfect tenses to show how actions are related in time. Study the chart.

Tense	When Do You Use It?	Examples
Present Perfect	For actions that began in the past and are still going on	Tensho **has helped** me since we became good friends.
	For actions that happened at an unknown past time	Our fathers **have worked** together a lot.
Past Perfect	For actions completed before another past action	Before I **met** Tensho, I **had hoped** to find a best friend.
Future Perfect	For actions that will happen before a future time	**By fall**, we **will have been** friends for two years.

Try It

A. Complete each sentence. Use one of the perfect tenses of the verb in parentheses.

1. Tensho _____ me for help. **(ask)**

2. He _____ me many times. **(help)**

3. I _____ to do something to repay him. **(want)**

4. Before Tensho's bike broke, he _____ it to get to his job after school. **(use)**

5. I _____ him my bike until his is repaired. **(offer)**

6. I _____ home from school all week. **(walk)**

7. By next weekend, the repair shop _____ his bike. **(fix)**

B. Choose words from each column to build five sentences about helping a friend. You can use words more than once.

Tensho I The repairman We	have been had been has helped has ridden will have fixed	the bike by Saturday. me many times. best friends for two years. worried about getting to work. my bike all week.

8. _____

9. _____

10. _____

11. _____

12. _____

Write It

C. Answer the questions about yourself and a good friend. Use perfect tenses.

13. How has your friend shown generosity when you needed help? _____

14. How will you have helped a friend by the end of the school year? _____

   _____

15. Have you learned to trust your friend, based on his or her actions? Why or why not?

   _____

D. (16–20) Write at least five sentences to tell about ways that you and a friend help each other. Use perfect tenses in your sentences.

   _____

   _____

   _____

   _____

   _____

101 Can a Verb Act Like an Adjective?

Yes, When It is a Participle

- Verbs have **four principal parts**. For example:

Present	Present Participle	Past	Past Participle
drive	driving	drove	driven
excite	exciting	excited	excited

- Many **verbs** are made up of a **helping verb** and a **participle**.
  Present Participle: My mother **is driving** to the store again.
  Past Participle: She **has driven** around all morning getting supplies.

- A **participle** can act as an adjective to describe a noun or pronoun.

  Mr. Powell is a **driven** man who tirelessly helps his neighbors.

  Excited, the neighbors look forward to the block party.

Try It

A. Combine sentences. Move the underlined participle to tell about a noun or a pronoun in the other sentence. Write the new sentence.

1. Warm weather brings the neighbors outside. They are <u>waiting</u>.

   _____

2. The neighbors set up tables and chairs. They are <u>excited</u>.

   _____

3. The block party includes new and old neighbors. It is <u>welcoming</u>.

   _____

4. The children greet their friends. They are <u>running</u>.

   _____

5. The teenagers form a large group. They are <u>dancing</u>.

   _____

B. Complete each sentence. Use the present participle or the past participle of the verb in parentheses as an adjective.

6. _____, Betsy asks Joey to perform. **(smile)**

7–8. _____, Joey sings. **(thrill)** The _____ crowd listens. **(please)**

9. _____, the neighbors praise Joey's performance. **(clap)**

Write It

C. Answer the questions. Use present and past participles as adjectives.

10. What yearly celebration or tradition do you enjoy in your community? _____

_____

11. How do most people feel about the celebration? _____

_____

D. (12–16) Now write at least five sentences to tell more about the community event. Use participles as adjectives.

_____

_____

_____

_____

Edit It

E. (17–20) Edit the letter below. Fix the four mistakes. Use present or past participles.

Dear Nora,

Today, our neighborhood had an exciting street fair. We thought it might be ruined by the drive winds. Grin, Mr. Pearson said not to worry. A band played boom rock music. We got there early. Exhaust, we finally left at 5 o'clock!

Your pal,

Ali

Proofreader's Marks

Change text:

Shouting
~~Shout~~ he called me over.

See all Proofreader's Marks on page ix.

102 What Are Participial Phrases?

Phrases That Start with a Participle

- A **participle** is a verb form, but it can act like an adjective to describe a noun or a pronoun. It can stand alone or come at the start of a **phrase**. A participle often ends in **-ing**.

  Working, Maria helps clean up trash in the neighborhood.

  Seeing the activity, Thomas joins the people **cleaning** the neighborhood.

- You can create a **participial phrase** to combine two sentences. If the phrase begins a sentence, use a comma (**,**) after the phrase.

  Maria helps with the clean-up. Maria works hard.

  Helping with the clean-up, Maria works hard.

- Place a participial phrase close to the noun or pronoun that it describes.

  Not OK: Thomas picks up soda bottles **bending** over the curb.

  OK: **Bending** over the curb, Thomas picks up soda bottles.

Try It

A. Use a participial phrase to combine sentences. Write the new sentence. Don't forget the comma after a participial phrase at the start of a sentence.

1. Mr. Rummel organizes the clean-up. Mr. Rummel assigns each neighbor a job.

   _____

2. Mrs. Rummel greets each neighbor. Mrs. Rummel hands out tools and garbage bags.

   _____

3. Thomas roams the neighborhood. Thomas gathers lots of bottles and cans.

   _____

4. Maria watches people. They are picking up paper and other debris.

   _____

5. Delia smiles as she works. Delia plants many flowers.

   _____

B. Choose from the participles in the box to complete each sentence.

exhausted	giggling	helping	looking	resting	sweeping

6. _____, Mr. Rodriguez sleeps in a chair.

7. Mrs. Rummel watches the children _____ with the clean-up.

8. _____ the sidewalk, Mrs. Bianco meets her neighbors.

9. She notices the whole neighborhood _____ much better.

10. _____, the adults admire the successful clean-up.

11. _____, the children race around the tidy playground.

Write It

C. Answer the questions about keeping neighborhoods clean. Use participial phrases in your answers.

12. Is there a clean-up in your neighborhood every year? _____

13. What kinds of jobs do people do in a neighborhood clean-up? _____
    _____

14. Is it important for people to work together to keep their neighborhood looking nice? Why or why not? _____
    _____

15. How does having a clean neighborhood benefit the people who live there? _____
    _____

D. (16–20) Write at least five sentences to tell more about how you and your neighbors keep your neighborhood clean. Use participial phrases in your sentences.

_____

_____

_____

_____

_____

103 How Can You Add Details to Your Sentences?

Use a Participial Phrase.

- A **participial phrase** begins with a **participle**.
  It acts like an adjective to describe a noun or a pronoun.

  1. The present participle for all verbs ends in **-ing**.

  Growing each year, my city has people from many countries.

  2. The past participle of a regular verb ends in **-ed**.
  An irregular verb has a special form.

Verb	Past	Past Participle
appreciate	appreciated	appreciated
choose	chose	chosen

  This neighborhood is a community **appreciated for its diversity**.

  Chosen by the community, our mayor is Chinese.

- You can use a participial phrase to add details to your sentences.
  Emigrating from Argentina, my father moved here three years ago.

Try It

A. Add a participial phrase to each sentence. Change the verb in parentheses to a present or past participle to start the phrase.

1. Our street has many buildings _____. **(inhabit)**

2. Mrs. Carvalho is a samba dancer _____. **(respect)**

3. _____, people have varied backgrounds. **(come)**

4. _____, the children learn about different cultures. **(share)**

5. Tina taught us a game _____. **(play)**

B. Complete each sentence about a diverse community. Use the correct form of the participle.

6. _____ their favorite foods, my classmates present dishes from their
   Cooking/Cooked
   cultures.

7. Badia's family brings us couscous _____ with vegetables.
   mixing/mixed

8. _____ stories about her grandmother, Sophia serves us pasta.
   Telling/Told

9. Dien gives us dumplings _____ in Vietnam.
   eating/eaten

10. I bring steak _____ Argentinean style.
    preparing/prepared

11. _____ with spices, Romero's pastries are delicious.
    Filling/Filled

Write It

C. Answer the questions about people in your community. Use participial phrases.

12. What cultures are represented in your community? _____

_____

13. What new foods have friends from other cultures shared with you? _____

_____

14. What foods would you share from your culture? _____

_____

15. What other aspects of your heritage would you share with your community? _____

_____

**D. (16–20) Write at least five sentences to tell more about the benefits of living
in a multicultural community. Use participial phrases.**

_____

_____

_____

_____

_____

104 What Is a "Dangling Participle"?

It's a Participle That Describes the Wrong Word.

- Always place a **participial phrase** by the word it describes.
  Sometimes you can just move the phrase to fix the problem.

  Not OK: I have lived here a long time, **finding this city wonderful**.

  OK: **Finding this city wonderful,** I have lived here a long time.

- Sometimes you need to rephrase the sentence and include a word for the participle to describe.

  Not OK: **Watching soccer,** our city's players had skills.

  OK: **Watching soccer,** Katya saw the skills of our city's players.

Try It

A. Fix each dangling participle. Write the sentence correctly.

1. Katya tells us about the soccer team beaming with pride.

_____

2. She shows us pictures of the winning goal returning from the latest game.

_____

_____

3. We recognized a player from our neighborhood looking at the pictures.

_____

_____

4. The coach unites the players believing in teamwork.

_____

5. The soccer team is everyone's favorite winning the championship.

_____

_____

6. Cheering at games, our team wins.

_____

B. (7-11) Complete each sentence. Make sure you have included a word or words for the participle to describe.

Kicking deftly, _____ the ball has reached the goal.

Screaming wildly, _____ the game is won. Running across

the field, _____ the crowd is happy. Breathing a sigh

of relief, _____ his team is elated. Bursting with pride,

_____ their son is a great soccer player.

Write It

C. Answer the questions about sports and other events that bring your community together. Use participial phrases correctly.

12. What sports events make you proud of your community? _____

_____

13. What other events (holidays, other traditional celebrations, and so on) in your community are you proud of? _____

_____

14. Do most people in your community attend these events? _____

_____

15. Describe your favorite community event. _____

_____

D. (16–20) Write at least five sentences to tell about one or more community events that you are proud of. Use participial phrases correctly.

_____

_____

_____

_____

_____

(105) Enrich Your Sentences

Remember: A **participle** is a verb form that can act as an adjective.
A **participial phrase** begins with a participle. Participles and participial phrases describe nouns and pronouns.

- A **participle** ends in **-ing** or **-ed**, or it has a special form. It can stand alone, or it can come at the start of a **participial phrase**.
  Worried new students enter the classroom.
  Showing friendliness, my classmates welcomed the refugees.
  Amazed by their new surroundings, the students explore the school.

- You can use participial phrases to combine or expand sentences.
  I admired the new students. I wanted to get to know them better.
  Admiring the new students, I wanted to get to know them better.

Try It

A. Use a participial phrase to combine each pair of sentences.

1. Nina left her grandparents. She emigrated from Bosnia. _____
_____

2. She was filled with sadness. She missed her homeland. _____
_____

3. Ahmed arrived from Africa. He quickly learned English. _____
_____

4. We were inspired by their courage. Everyone rallied around the new students. _____
_____

B. Complete each sentence about new students. Use the correct form of the participle.

5. _____ slowly, Nina tells us her story.
      Talking / Talked

6. _____ together, Nina and Ahmed discuss their new school.
      Sitting / Sat

7. Ahmed is a friendly teen _____ for his humor.
                              knowing / known

233

Write It

C. Answer the questions about an inspiring student. Tell how you are inspired by this person. Use participles and participial phrases correctly.

8. Is there a student in your school whom you find especially inspiring? _____

_____

9. What makes this person so remarkable? _____

_____

10. What is a fascinating detail about this person's life? _____

_____

D. (11–14) Write at least four sentences to tell about an inspiring student. Use participles and participial phrases.

_____

_____

_____

_____

Edit It

E. (15–20) Edit the letter. Fix the six mistakes with participles.

Dear Parents and Students:

Building on last year's success, the Student Outreach Group has had another tremendous year. This year's students are a dynamic group distinguishing by their diversity. Represented seven countries, they bring new viewpoints to our community. Used their talents, our students tried to make newcomers feel welcome. Created opportunities for students to mingle was a priority. Describe as a home away from home, the Student Center is a success. Inspiring by new students, many older students have joined our group.

Sincerely yours,

Vice Principal Kristina Hagopian

Proofreader's Marks

Change text:

~~Surprising~~ Surprised by their welcome, the students smiled.

See all Proofreader's Marks on page ix.